Capilano College Library

D0578251

INTRODUCTIONS TO
MODERN ENGLISH LITERATURE
FOR STUDENTS OF ENGLISH

Modern Short Stories

Alex Martin and Robert Hill

ENGLISH LANGUAGE TEACHING

Prentice Hall

New York London Toronto Sydney Tokyo Singapore

Published 1992 by
Prentice Hall International (UK) Limited
Campus 400, Maylands Avenue
Hemel Hempstead, Hertfordshire
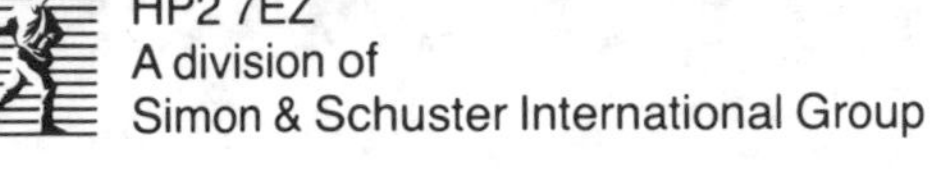
HP2 7EZ
A division of
Simon & Schuster International Group

First published 1991 by Cassell Publishers Limited

Typeset by Litho Link Ltd, Welshpool, Powys, Wales
Design by Derek Lee
Cover illustration by Jim Woods

Printed in Great Britain by Redwood Books, Trowbridge, Wiltshire

This book is affectionately dedicated to
Audrey and Peter Hill

British Library Cataloguing in Publication Data

Information available from the Publisher on request

ISBN 0-13-481805-9

4 5 96 95 94

Acknowledgements

The Editors and Publishers would like to thank the following for their kind permission to reproduce the following copyright texts:

Heinemann Octopus for *Under the Banyan Tree* by R K Narayan; Chatto and Windus for *The Nice and the Good* by Iris Murdoch; Warner Chappell Music Ltd for *They can't take that away from me* by G and I Gershwin; Peters Fraser and Dunlop Group Ltd for *First Confession* by F O'Connor; Random Century Group for *A Portrait of the Artist as a Young Man* by J Joyce, and *The Natural* and *The First Seven Years* by B Malamud; Andre Deutsch Ltd for *Ace in the Hole* by J Updike and for definitions from *A Dictionary of Literary Terms* by J A Cuddon; Barry Cole for *Reported Missing* by B Cole; Hamish Hamilton Ltd for *The Little Girl and the Wolf* by J Thurber; Murray Pollinger for 'Lamb to the Slaughter' from *Someone Like You* by Roald Dahl; Oxford University Press for definitions from A S Hornby's *Oxford Advanced Learner's Dictionary* (4th Edition 1989).

We are grateful to the following for permission to reproduce pictures:

By courtesy of the Trustees of the Victoria and Albert Museum *Luncheon (Deux Belges)* by John Copley p 30; The Hulton-Deutsch Collection pp 45, 62, 65, 77, 91, 121 and 135; Country Life p 10; Maggie Murray/Format *Village Council* p 17; Tate Gallery, London for *Beata Beatrix* p 80; Mary Evans Picture Library p 101.

Contents

Introduction

1. To The Student

This book is for those who either want to read some English short stories or have to read some for school, university or exams. You don't need to have studied literature before. The aim of the book is to help you understand and enjoy reading short stories, and so to give you tools and methods for appreciating stories you read in the future.

You can use the book with or without a teacher. If you are studying alone, you will need to check your answers in the Key at the end of the book. As the study of literature sometimes requires a purely personal response, however, not all the exercises have a single correct answer. In these cases it would be useful to discuss your ideas with a teacher, and it would certainly be interesting to discuss your ideas with a friend or another student.

The books in this series adopt a double approach: literary and linguistic. Each chapter contains a Language section divided into Language Practice and Vocabulary, in addition to the section on Close Reading. The Language section is always based on the literature in that chapter, and in almost all cases leads back into it. The result is that the two approaches 'feed' each other: the linguistic study helping you to appreciate the literature, and the literature helping you to appreciate (and use) the language.

After the Language section in each chapter there is a section called Extension, which gives you the chance to discuss or write about themes raised by the stories. A final section, Beyond the Text, offers you another piece of literature which compares or contrasts with what you have read in the chapter, showing other treatments of the same theme.

You can work on the chapters in any order you like, but we suggest that you begin at least with Chapter 1. This is because the two short stories in Chapter 1 deal with the art of story-telling, and because you are introduced to some of the basic features of plot. Other useful ideas to enable you to talk confidently about stories are introduced in Chapter 2 (metaphor and simile) and Chapter 3 (narrator and point of view).

Finally, in order to make the best of this book, you should (indeed must) have (1) a good monolingual English dictionary, (2) a good bilingual dictionary, and (3) a handbook of English grammar and usage. You may also (4) want to know more about the historical and cultural background to the stories you read here. The following is a basic list of suggestions to cover these necessities:

(1) *Oxford Advanced Learner's Dictionary* or *Longman Dictionary of Contemporary English.*

(2) This will depend on what is available, but buy a large, modern dictionary if possible. Ask the advice of someone who knows both languages well. A good dictionary is a marvellous intellectual tool which will serve you for many years. It should (a) translate a large number of words, (b) give all the possible meanings for these words, and (c) reflect past as well as modern usage. Avoid mini-dictionaries, therefore, which have their place in the tourist's suitcase but are useless for the study of literature.

(3) Jake Allsop, *Cassell's Students' English Grammar* (Cassell)
A J Thomson & A V Martinet, *A Practical English Grammar* (Oxford)
Raymond Murphy, *English Grammar in Use* (Cambridge)
Michael Swan, *Practical English Usage* (Oxford).

(4) Harry Blamires, *Twentieth Century English Literature* (Macmillan)
Boris Ford (editor), *The Pelican Guide to English Literature,* Volumes 7 and 8 (Penguin).

At the back of the book you will find a Glossary. In this section are listed the most essential vocabulary items for each story, together with words and phrases which are not usually included in a standard dictionary, such as slang and dialect. These words are listed in the order they appear in the text, rather than in alphabetical order.

2. To The Teacher

Little needs to be added except to note that, although the book is written with private study in mind, practically every exercise in the book will work in the classroom with little or no adaptation. Many of the individual exercises can be transformed by the addition of simple instructions: 'discuss' (in pairs or groups), 'report your conclusions', etc. As the use of literature in the language class is still something of a novelty, however (albeit a rediscovered one), it's worth pointing out that the application of communicative teaching techniques to the study of literature can, with a bit of imagination and flexibility, produce excellent results. Time spent on thinking up suitable ways to introduce games, dramatisation, surveys, quizzes, puzzles, debates, role-plays and projects — all of which (provided they are relevant) will motivate the student further — will almost always pay handsome returns. But in setting up any group activity (especially a discussion), it is essential to give the student a specific goal — a decision to be reached, in a specific time. The approach of 'discuss Question Four', followed inevitably by 'discuss Question Five' is not likely to be much of a success in any context.

The *while reading* questions that occur during the short stories can be done in pairs, groups, or as class brainstorming. They are there to:
a) give the students achievable portions of texts to read
b) encourage the students to engage in the mechanics of the plot
c) aid, rather than test, comprehension by highlighting the questions that a practised reader would be asking him/herself.

These questions should therefore be dealt with fairly rapidly, and the students should carry on reading the story at the first sign of the class discussion or pair/group work flagging. A more leisurely and deeper analysis of the story is always provided for in the Close reading section.

The First reaction question should also be dealt with quickly. The rationale behind this question is to harness that moment when any reader (even the least practised) tends to want to make a subjective response. We hope that this question will encourage the less confident students to begin to make assertions about their reactions to stories. Any discussion of these assertions, however, should be left till after the Close reading when students will have looked at key moments in the story and should be able to take a more informed critical stance.

Finally, if you find yourself disagreeing violently with the answers in the Key, you can of course treat them as further discussion points. It is probably unwise to suggest that all the literary questions are debatable, but a good many certainly are, at least to the extent that there is more to be said.

Robert Hill
Alex Martin

1 Short Stories and Tall Tales

THE OPEN WINDOW
'Saki' (H H Munro)

Before you read

1 These are some common expressions used when talking about short stories. Match them with the definitions below.

a) suspense	**b)** surprise	**c)** plot	**d)** character(s)
e) setting	**f)** climax	**g)** theme	**h)** style

i) the manner of writing used in the story. __

ii) the feeling in the reader caused by something unexpected happening. __

iii) the place and time at which the events of a story take place. __

iv) the set of connected events on which a story is based. __

v) what the story is *about,* rather than what happens in the story. __

vi) a tense feeling in the reader, caused by wondering what may happen. __

vii) the most intense part of a story, generally towards the end. __

viii) a person (or people) in a story. __

2 Use the expressions in the box in question 1 to fill in the gaps in these sentences. In each case decide if the sentence makes a positive or negative comment.

i) The story is too simple to be interesting: the ___________ are too neatly divided into good and bad.

ii) I found the ___________ too complicated: at times it was difficult to understand what was going on.

iii) ___________ is maintained throughout this thrilling story: you don't find out the identity of the murderer until the last page, and when you do, it comes as a complete ___________.

iv) Very little actually happens in this story – it is an ordinary day in the life of an ordinary person – but the writer's ___________ makes it fascinating reading.

v) In spite of the exotic ____________, in India at the time of the Mogul Emperors, the story is rather dull.

vi) The story's ____________, racial intolerance in an urban setting, makes it still relevant for today's reader.

vii) The writer builds up the reader's expectations skilfully, but the ____________ itself is rather disappointing.

3 Are there any stories or novels you have read recently about which you would make similar comments?

The Open Window

'My aunt will be down presently, Mr. Nuttel,' said a very self-possessed young lady of fifteen; 'in the meantime you must try and put up with me.'

Framton Nuttel endeavoured to say the correct something which should duly flatter the niece of the moment without unduly discounting the aunt that was to come. Privately he doubted more than ever whether these formal visits on a succession of total strangers would do much towards helping the nerve cure which he was supposed to be undergoing. 5

'I know how it will be,' his sister had said when he was preparing to migrate to this rural retreat; 'you will bury yourself down there and not speak to a living soul, and your nerves will be worse than ever from moping. I shall just give you letters of introduction to all the people I know there. Some of them, as far as I can remember, were quite nice.' 10

Framton wondered whether Mrs. Sappleton, the lady to whom he was presenting one of the letters of introduction, came into the nice division. 15

'Do you know many of the people round here?' asked the niece, when she judged that they had had sufficient silent communion.

'Hardly a soul,' said Framton. 'My sister was staying here, at the rectory, you know, some four years ago, and she gave me letters of introduction to some of the people here.' 20

He made the last statement in a tone of distinct regret.

'Then you know practically nothing about my aunt?' pursued the self-possessed young lady.

'Only her name and address,' admitted the caller. He was wondering whether Mrs. Sappleton was in the married or widowed state. An undefinable something about the room seemed to suggest masculine habitation. 25

'Her great tragedy happened just three years ago,' said the child; 'that would be since your sister's time.' 30

'Her tragedy?' asked Framton; somehow in this restful country spot tragedies seemed out of place.

What might this 'tragedy' be? Try to think of two or three possibilities.

'You may wonder why we keep that window wide open on an October afternoon,' said the niece, indicating a large French window that opened on to a lawn. 35

'It is quite warm for the time of the year,' said Framton; 'but has that window got anything to do with the tragedy?'

'Out through that window, three years ago to a day, her husband and her two young brothers went off for their day's shooting. They never came back. In crossing the moor to their favourite snipe-shooting ground 40 they were all three engulfed in a treacherous piece of bog. It had been that dreadful wet summer, you know, and places that were safe in other years gave way suddenly without warning. Their bodies were never recovered. That was the dreadful part of it.' Here the child's voice lost its self-possessed note and became falteringly human. 'Poor aunt always 45 thinks that they will come back some day, they and the little brown spaniel that was lost with them, and walk in at that window just as they used to do. That is why the window is kept open every evening till it is quite dusk. Poor dear aunt, she has often told me how they went out, her husband with his white waterproof coat over his arm, and Ronnie, 50 her youngest brother, singing, "Bertie, why do you bound?" as he always did to tease her, because she said it got on her nerves. Do you know, sometimes on still, quiet evenings like this, I almost get a creepy feeling that they will all walk in through that window—'

She broke off with a little shudder. It was a relief to Framton when the 55 aunt bustled into the room with a whirl of apologies for being late in making her appearance.

'I hope Vera has been amusing you?' she said.

'She has been very interesting,' said Framton.

'I hope you don't mind the open window,' said Mrs. Sappleton 60 briskly; 'my husband and brothers will be home directly from shooting, and they always come in this way. They've been out for snipe in the marshes to-day, so they'll make a fine mess over my poor carpets. So like you men-folk, isn't it?'

She rattled on cheerfully about the shooting and the scarcity of birds, 65 and the prospects for duck in the winter. To Framton it was all purely horrible. He made a desperate but only partially successful effort to turn the talk on to a less ghastly topic; he was conscious that his hostess was giving him only a fragment of her attention, and her eyes were constantly straying past him to the open window and the lawn beyond. 70 It was certainly an unfortunate coincidence that he should have paid his visit on this tragic anniversary.

'The doctors agree in ordering me complete rest, an absence of mental excitement, and avoidance of anything in the nature of violent physical exercise,' announced Framton, who laboured under the tolerably 75 widespread delusion that total strangers and chance acquaintances are hungry for the least detail of one's ailments and infirmities, their cause and cure. 'On the matter of diet they are not so much in agreement,' he continued.

'No?' said Mrs. Sappleton, in a voice which only replaced a yawn at the last moment. Then she suddenly brightened into alert attention – but not to what Framton was saying.

'Here they are at last!' she cried. 'Just in time for tea, and don't they look as if they were muddy up to the eyes!'

Framton shivered slightly and turned towards the niece with a look intended to convey sympathetic comprehension. The child was staring out through the open window with dazed horror in her eyes. In a chill shock of nameless fear Framton swung round in his seat and looked in the same direction.

How does Framton feel at this moment?
How is the story going to develop now, do you think?

In the deepening twilight three figures were walking across the lawn towards the window; they all carried guns under their arms, and one of them was additionally burdened with a white coat hung over his shoulders. A tired brown spaniel kept close at their heels. Noiselessly they neared the house, and then a hoarse young voice chanted out of the dusk: 'I said, Bertie, why do you bound?'

Framton grabbed wildly at his stick and hat; the hall-door, the gravel-drive, and the front gate were dimly noted stages in his headlong retreat. A cyclist coming along the road had to run into the hedge to avoid imminent collision.

'Here we are, my dear,' said the bearer of the white mackintosh, coming in through the window; 'fairly muddy, but most of it's dry. Who was that who bolted out as we came up?'

'A most extraordinary man, a Mr. Nuttel,' said Mrs. Sappleton; 'could only talk about his illnesses, and dashed off without a word of good-bye or apology when you arrived. One would think he had seen a ghost.'

'I expect it was the spaniel,' said the niece calmly; 'he told me he had a horror of dogs. He was once hunted into a cemetery somewhere on the banks of the Ganges by a pack of pariah dogs, and had to spend the night in a newly dug grave with the creatures snarling and grinning and foaming just above him. Enough to make any one lose their nerve.'

Romance at short notice was her speciality.

See Glossary section at the back of the book for vocabulary.

First reaction

4 a) Do you find this story amusing, or not? Why?

b) Are the events of the story credible, or not? Does this matter very much?

Close reading

Analysing the plot

5 Analyse the plot of this story. For this story, and for other stories, the following scheme may be helpful for your analysis.

The setting
WHO are the main characters?
WHERE does the story take place?
WHEN does the story take place?
WHAT is the situation?
Has anything happened before the story begins?

THEN, WHAT happens?
What starts the events of the story moving?
WHAT happens as a result of that?
WHAT happens finally? What is the resolution?

The setting

WHO are the main characters?	The important characters are in the first few lines. **a)** ____________ **b)** ____________ **c)** ____________
WHERE does the story take place?	Which of these is correct? **a)** in town **b)** in a quiet place in the country
WHEN does the story take place?	Is there any indication that this is a story set in a historical period, or even in the future? Or do we assume that it takes place at the same time as the author wrote the story? Do you think it is particularly important for the effect of this story?
WHAT is the situation?	Has anything happened before the story begins? Framton Nuttel is recovering from ____________ His sister has ____________ ____________
WHAT happens next?	Look at lines 29-32. Mrs. Sappleton's niece ____________ ____________

WHAT happens as a result of that?	Look at lines 55-72. Who appears on the scene? What does she say? What is the resulting effect on Framton? When Mrs. ____________________ ____________________ she ____________________ ____________________ so Framton ____________________ ____________________
WHAT happens finally?	Look at lines 83-end. Mrs. Sappleton sees ____________________ ____________________ and Framton thinks ____________________ ____________________ ____________________ so he ____________________ ____________________ ____________________

6 Vera is a 'very self-possessed young lady' and a specialist in 'romance at short notice'. She is also very clever.

a) Why does she ask the question 'Then you know practically nothing about my aunt?' (line 23)?

b) When Mrs. Sappleton's husband and her brothers come back, what does she do to convince Framton even more that they are ghosts?

7 Use the scheme you used in question 5 to analyse briefly the story that Vera tells Framton.

Notice that there is no resolution to Vera's story, 'the story within the story'. Part of the amusing effect of Saki's story is that the resolution that one expects from Vera's story – the return of these men as ghosts – is transferred, for comic effect, into the main story.

UNDER THE BANYAN TREE
R K Narayan

Before you read

8 In the previous story, we saw the precocious Vera making up rather a 'black' story. The protagonist of the story you are going to read now is a very different kind of story-teller. He is a story-teller in an Indian village, who makes up stories based on traditional myths and legends.

a) What kind of characters do you think his stories might be about?

b) What do you think his social status is likely to be?

Under the Banyan Tree

The village Somal, nestling away in the forest tracts of Mempi, had a population of less than three hundred. It was in every way a village to make the heart of a rural reformer sink. Its tank, a small expanse of water, right in the middle of the village, served for drinking, bathing, and washing the cattle, and it bred malaria, typhoid, and heaven knew (5) what else. The cottages sprawled anyhow and the lanes twisted and wriggled up and down and strangled each other. The population used the highway as the refuse ground and in the backyard of every house drain water stagnated in green puddles.

Such was the village. It is likely that the people of the village were insensitive: but it is more than likely that they never noticed their surroundings because they lived in a kind of perpetual enchantment. The enchanter was Nambi the story-teller. He was a man of about sixty or seventy. Or was he eighty or one hundred and eighty? Who could say? In a place so much cut off as Somal (the nearest bus-stop was ten miles away), reckoning could hardly be in the familiar measures of time. If anyone asked Nambi what his age was he referred to an ancient famine or an invasion or the building of a bridge and indicated how high he had stood from the ground at the time.

He was illiterate, in the sense that the written word was a mystery to him; but he could make up a story, in his head, at the rate of one a month; each story took nearly ten days to narrate.

His home was the little temple which was at the very end of the village. No one could say how he had come to regard himself as the owner of the temple. The temple was a very small structure with red-striped walls, with a stone image of the Goddess Shakti in the sanctum. The front portion of the temple was Nambi's home. For aught it mattered any place might be his home; for he was without possessions. All that he possessed was a broom with which he swept the temple; and he had also a couple of dhoties and upper cloth. He spent most of the day in the shade of the banyan which spread out its branches in front of the temple. When he felt hungry he walked into any house that caught his fancy and joined the family at dinner. When he needed new clothes they were brought to him by the villagers. He hardly ever had to go out in search of company; for the banyan shade served as a clubhouse for the village folk. All through the day people came seeking Nambi's company and squatted under the tree. If he was in a mood for it he listened to their talk and entertained them with his own observations and anecdotes. When he was in no mood he looked at the visitors sourly and asked, 'What do you think I am? Don't blame me if you get no story at the next moon. Unless I meditate how can the Goddess give me a story? Do you think stories float in the air?' And he moved out to the edge of the forest and squatted there, contemplating the trees.

On Friday evenings the village turned up at the temple for worship, when Nambi lit a score of mud lamps and arranged them around the threshold of the sanctuary. He decorated the image with flowers, which grew wildly in the backyard of the temple. He acted as the priest and offered to the Goddess fruits and flowers brought in by the villagers.

On the nights he had a story to tell he lit a small lamp and placed it in a niche in the trunk of the banyan tree. Villagers as they returned home in the evening saw this, went home, and said to their wives, 'Now, now, hurry up with the dinner, the story-teller is calling us.' As the moon crept up behind the hillock, men, women, and children gathered under the banyan tree. The story-teller would not appear yet. He would be sitting in the sanctum, before the Goddess, with his eyes shut, in deep meditation. He sat thus as long as he liked and when he came out, with his forehead ablaze with ash and vermilion, he took his seat on a stone platform in front of the temple. He opened the story with a question.

What question do you think he will ask?

Jerking his finger towards a vague, far-away destination, he asked, 'A thousand years ago, a stone's throw in that direction, what do you think there was? It was not the weed covered waste it is now, for donkeys to roll in. It was not the ash-pit it is now. It was the capital of the king. . . .' The King would be Dasaratha, Vikramaditya, Asoka, or anyone that came into the old man's head; the capital was called Kapila, Kridapura, or anything. Opening thus, the old man went on without a pause for three hours. By then brick by brick the palace of the king was raised. The old man described the dazzling durbar hall where sat a hundred vassal kings, ministers, and subjects; in another part of the palace all the musicians in the world assembled and sang; and most of the songs were sung over again by Nambi to his audience; and he described in detail the pictures and trophies that hung on the walls of the palace. . . .

It was story-building on an epic scale. The first day barely conveyed the setting of the tale, and Nambi's audience as yet had no idea who were coming into the story. As the moon slipped behind the trees of Mempi Forest Nambi said, 'Now friends, Mother says this will do for the day.' He abruptly rose, went in, lay down, and fell asleep long before the babble of the crowd ceased.

The light in the niche would again be seen two or three days later, and again and again throughout the bright half of the month. Kings and heroes, villains and fairy-like women, gods in human form, saints and assassins, jostled each other in that world which was created under the banyan tree. Nambi's voice rose and fell in an exquisite rhythm, and the moonlight and the hour completed the magic. The villagers laughed with Nambi, they wept with him, they adored the heroes, cursed the villains, groaned when the conspirator had his initial success, and they sent up to the gods a heartfelt prayer for a happy ending. . . .

On the day when the story ended, the whole gathering went into the sanctum and prostrated before the Goddess. . . .

By the time the next moon peeped over the hillock Nambi was ready with another story. He never repeated the same kind of story or brought in the same set of persons, and the village folk considered Nambi a sort of miracle, quoted his words of wisdom, and lived on the whole in an exalted plane of their own, though their life in all other respects was hard and drab.

And yet it had gone on for years and years. One moon he lit the lamp in the tree. The audience came. The old man took his seat and began the story. '. . . When King Vikramaditya lived, his minister was . . .' He paused. He could not get beyond it. He made a fresh beginning. 'There was the king . . .' he said, repeated it, and then his words trailed off into a vague mumbling. 'What has come over me?' he asked pathetically. 'Oh, Mother, great Mother, why do I stumble and falter? I know the story. I had the whole of it a moment ago. What was it about? I can't understand what has happened.' He faltered and looked so miserable that his audience said, 'Take your own time. You are perhaps tired.' 105

'Shut up!' he cried. 'Am I tired? Wait a moment; I will tell you the story presently.' Following this there was utter silence. Eager faces looked up at him. 'Don't look at me!' he flared up. Somebody gave him a tumbler of milk. The audience waited patiently. This was a new experience. Some persons expressed their sympathy aloud. Some persons began to talk among themselves. Those who sat in the outer edge of the crowd silently slipped away. Gradually, as it neared midnight, others followed this example. Nambi sat staring at the ground, his head bowed in thought. For the first time he realized that he was old. He felt he would never more be able to control his thoughts or express them cogently. He looked up. Everyone had gone except his friend Mari the blacksmith. 'Mari, why aren't you also gone?' 110 115

Mari apologized for the rest: 'They didn't want to tire you; so they have gone away.' 120

Nambi got up. 'You are right. Tomorrow I will make it up. Age, age. What is my age? It has come on suddenly.' He pointed at his head and said, 'This says, "Old fool, don't think I shall be your servant any more. You will be my servant hereafter." It is disobedient and treacherous.'

He lit the lamp in the niche next day. The crowd assembled under the banyan faithfully. Nambi had spent the whole day in meditation. He had been fervently praying to the Goddess not to desert him. He began the story. He went on for an hour without a stop. He felt greatly relieved, so much so that he interrupted his narration to remark, 'Oh, friends, The Mother is always kind. I was seized with a foolish fear . . .' and continued the story. In a few minutes he felt dried up. He struggled hard: 'And then . . . and then . . . what happened?' He stammered. There followed a pause lasting an hour. The audience rose without a word and went home. The old man sat on the stone brooding till the cock crew. 'I can't blame them for it,' he muttered to himself. 'Can they sit down here and mope all night?' Two days later he gave another instalment of the story, and that, too, lasted only a few minutes. The gathering dwindled. Fewer persons began to take notice of the lamp in the niche. Even these came only out of a sense of duty. Nambi realized that there was no use in prolonging the struggle. He brought the story to a speedy and premature end. 125 130 135 140

He knew what was happening. He was harrowed by the thoughts of his failure. I should have been happier if I had dropped dead years ago, he said to himself. Mother, why have you struck me dumb . . .? He shut himself up in the sanctum, hardly ate any food, and spent the greater part of the day sitting motionless in meditation. 145

How is the story going to develop now, do you think?

The next moon peeped over the hillock, Nambi lit the lamp in the niche. The villagers as they returned home saw the lamp, but only a handful turned up at night. 'Where are the others?' the old man asked. 'Let us wait.' He waited. The moon came up. His handful of audience waited patiently. And then the old man said, 'I won't tell the story today, nor tomorrow unless the whole village comes here. I insist upon it. It is a mighty story. Everyone must hear it.' Next day he went up and down the village street shouting, 'I have a most wonderful tale to tell tonight. Come one and all; don't miss it. . . .' This personal appeal had a great effect. At night a large crowd gathered under the banyan. They were happy that the story-teller had regained his powers. Nambi came out of the temple when everyone had settled and said. 'It is the Mother who gives the gifts; and it is she who takes away the gifts. Nambi is a dotard. He speaks when the Mother has anything to say. He is struck dumb when she has nothing to say. But what is the use of the jasmine when it has lost its scent? What is the lamp for when all the oil is gone? Goddess be thanked. . . . These are my last words on this earth; and this is my greatest story.' He rose and went into the sanctum. His audience hardly understood what he meant. They sat there till they became weary. And then some of them got up and stepped into the sanctum. There the story-teller sat with eyes shut. 'Aren't you going to tell us a story?' they asked. He opened his eyes, looked at them, and shook his head. He indicated by gesture that he had spoken his last words. 150 155 160 165

When he felt hungry he walked into any cottage and silently sat down for food, and walked away the moment he had eaten. Beyond this he had hardly anything to demand of his fellow beings. The rest of his life (he lived for a few more years) was one great consummate silence. 170

See Glossary section at the back of the book for vocabulary.

First reaction

9 How do you feel at the end of this story? You can choose more than one reaction, or write your own.

Interested:	this story seems to raise interesting questions.
Disappointed:	the story seems to build up to a climax and then nothing happens.
Satisfied:	this is the only ending possible.
Bored:	nothing happens.

Your reaction: ______________________________

Close reading

Analysing the plot

10 Analyse the plot of this story in the same way as you did for the story by 'Saki'.

The setting

WHO are the main characters?	Try to summarise in one sentence what we are told about Nambi. Do the same for the villagers.
WHERE does the story take place?	Try to summarise in one sentence what we are told about the village.
WHEN does the story take place?	
WHAT is the situation? Has anything happened before the story begins?	What sort of relationship exists between Nambi and the villagers?
WHAT happens next?	**i)** Identify the paragraph, and **ii)** try to specify sentences within the paragraph.
WHAT happens as a result of that?	How does Nambi react?
WHAT happens finally?	______________________
What is the resolution?	______________________

11 Why was Nambi such a successful story-teller?

12 Where and how does Narayan use *suspense* and *surprise*?

13 The similarity between Saki's story and Narayan's story is that the main character in both is a prolific story-teller, although one is at the beginning of her career, the other at the end! But there are important differences. Saki's story is simply a story meant to amuse. Narayan's story, on the other hand, seems to be about something serious: some kind of comment on life is implied.

Look at lines 115-24, 142-6, 157-64. Does anything seem to be suggested about growing old?

Language practice

Using different tenses in narrative – past simple + past perfect tense (*had* + past participle)

"My aunt will be down presently, Mr. Nuttel," said a very self-possessed young lady of fifteen . . ."

"I know how it will be" his sister, had said when he was preparing to migrate to this rural retreat . . . *The Open Window* (lines 1-2; 10-11).

'And yet it had gone on for years and years. One moon he lit the lamp in the tree.' *Under the Banyan Tree* (line 96).

14 Why are the underlined verbs in different tenses?

15 If we examine stories as pieces of 'real life' set in real time, we can see an obvious *chronological sequence* of events: one thing happens before another, then another thing happens and then another, and so on. Yet in novels, stories, anecdotes, jokes – in fact, any kind of story-telling – the sequence of events in real time is often changed in order to make the story more dramatic; events are presented to us in a *narrative sequence* rather than a chronological sequence.

For example, the events presented to the reader at the beginning of Saki's story would be in this order in a chronological sequence:

a) Framton's sister visits some people in the country.
b) Framton has a nervous breakdown.
c) Framton's sister gives Framton the addresses of the people she visited in the country so he can visit them.
d) Framton goes to the house of one of these people.
e) The first person he meets is the niece of the person he is supposed to visit.
f) The niece asks him if he knows the people around there.

But at which point does Saki begin his story? In what order are we told about these events – what is the narrative sequence?

1. ___ 2. ___ 3. ___
4. ___ 5. ___ 6. ___

16 In the following 'tall story' (a highly incredible story) put the verbs in brackets into either the past simple or the past perfect tense.

Nigel Timms was an ambitious young executive. Recently, his boss, Mr Sharkey, (**1** start) __________ talking about promotion, so, for obvious reasons, Nigel (**2** invite) __________ the Sharkeys to dinner. As it was near Christmas, Nigel and his wife Charlotte (**3** decide) ________ on roast turkey for their guests.

On Friday evening the guests (**4** arrive) ________. Charlotte, although she (**5** spend) ________ most of the day shopping and cooking, was looking lovely. When the first course was over Charlotte (**6** go) ________ into the kitchen to get the roast turkey, which she (**7** take) ________ out of the oven just before serving the soup. But something terrible (**8** happen) ________! Smudge, their cat, had been enjoying his own Christmas dinner. In fact, he (**9** already eat) ________ most of one leg and was now starting on the other. Charlotte immediately kicked him out into the garden and then (**10** wonder) ________ what to do next. She (**11** certainly not want) ________ to ruin the meal, which (**12** take) ________ her hours to prepare, or her husband's chances of promotion, so she decided to keep quiet. She (**13** carve) ________ the turkey in the kitchen so that no-one would see the damage that Smudge (**14** do) ________.

The turkey (**15** be) ________ a great success, so, by the time Charlotte (**16** go) ________ into the kitchen to make coffee she (**17** completely forgive) ________ Smudge, and (**18** open) ________ the back door to let him in again. But something even worse than before (**19** happen) ________! There, on the doorstep, was the dead body of poor Smudge. Charlotte (**20** be) ________ horrified as she worked out what (**21** happen) ________: Smudge (**22** obviously die) ________ of food poisoning . . . and their guests (**23** eat) ________ the turkey too!

She (**24** call) ________ Nigel into the kitchen and (**25** tell) ________ him everything. After much discussion, they decided to tell their guests the whole story. They all (**26** agree) ________ that the only thing to do was to go to the hospital and have the turkey pumped out of their stomachs.

After this unpleasant operation, they (**27** say) ________ goodbye outside the hospital. 'Thanks for an unforgettable evening!' said Mr Sharkey, ironically. The Timms went sadly home, and (**28** go) ________ in through the back gate to pick up the body of poor Smudge. It was then that they (**29** see) ________ a note on the ground, which Charlotte (**30** not notice) ________ before. It was from their next door neighbour, and said, 'I'm very sorry about your cat, but there was nothing I could do! It jumped in front of my car while I was driving out of my garage. I can see that you have guests, so I'm leaving this note instead of ringing your doorbell so as not to ruin your evening.'

Would this story be the same if the narrative sequence was the same as the chronological sequence? What would be different?

17 The following events from a thriller in the style of a James Bond story are listed in chronological sequence.

- Bond said goodnight to Tatania.
- He went up to his hotel room.
- He switched on the light.
- He saw Olga sitting on his bed.
- Someone hit him hard on the head.
- He fell unconscious to the floor.
- Someone tied him to the bed.

▶ He woke up.

- His head was aching.
- He tried to move but found he couldn't.
- He remembered what had happened the night before.
- He wondered where Olga was now.

Use the guide below to write a paragraph in narrative sequence beginning at the ▶ symbol.

Bond ____________. His head ____________. He ______ to move but ________________________. Someone ________________________ __________ bed! Then ____________________________ night before. He ____________________________ and had __________ ____________ hotel room. He ____________________________ and seen ____________________ bed. Then ______________________ _______ head and he ____________________________ floor. He ________________________ now.

18 Write two or three sentences to finish the following paragraph.

When Cynthia finally regained consciousness she was in the back of a moving truck. All around her there were boxes with strange writing on them. Then she remembered . . .

Vocabulary

Describing types of stories

19 Short stories can be set anywhere and at any time; they can involve all kinds of characters, and can be about anything at all. There is no reason why we should classify all short stories into types. This would be extremely difficult to do, particularly with the best short stories, whose subtlety and thematic interest make them unique. However, particularly among more 'popular' short stories, whose aim is principally to entertain the reader rather than to raise interesting questions about life, we can distinguish various types (sometimes called *genres:* pronounced /'ʒɑːnrəz/). Look at these various genres and use your dictionary to look up any expressions you don't know. In the list there are also some kinds of story that are usually told orally, and not written down.

> detective story spy story travelogue fairy story ghost story
> adventure story myth tear-jerker story with social significance
> folk-tale thriller humorous story science-fiction story legend
> crime story romantic story spine-chiller anecdote Western
> horror story whodunnit parable tall story love story joke

20 a) Which of the above are usually oral: that is, people usually tell them to each other rather than write them down?

b) Can you think of some examples of the above genres by English writers and from your own culture?

c) Which of the genres above are similar to each other in that they have the same kind of setting and same kind of main characters?

d) Which of these genres do you like? Which do you never read? Can you explain your preferences?

Extension

21 Which of the two stories in this chapter did you prefer? Why?

22 Can you remember any stories you were told when you were young? What did you find appealing about them, and why do you remember them?

23 'The cinema, and more recently television, have completely replaced the need for oral and written stories.' Do you agree?

24 Write a story in about 200/250 words. It could be something amusing, frightening or in some way interesting that has happened to you; a story someone has told you; or you could re-tell a story that you have read or the plot of a film that has particularly impressed you.

Beyond the text

A story from a novel

In this extract from *The Nice and The Good* by Iris Murdoch (1968) Willy, a Jewish refugee from Eastern Europe, reveals a little of his past to Mary, a woman who has fallen in love with him.

25 What seems to be the point of Willy's story? What does it say about life?

'We were on a summer holiday,' Willy went on, 'at a seaside place on the Black Sea. Every morning I went with my nurse into the public gardens and she sat down and knitted and I pretended to play. I didn't really play because I didn't know how to play like that in public and I was frightened of other children. I knew I was supposed to run about 5
and I ran about and pretended to pretend to be a horse. But all the time I was worrying in case someone should look at me and know that it was all false and that I was not a happy child playing at all, but a little frightened thing running to and fro. I would have liked just to sit quietly beside my nurse, but she would not allow that and would tell me to run 10
about and enjoy myself. There were other children in the public gardens but they were mostly older than me and went about in groups of their own. Then one day a little fair-haired girl with a small black and white dog came to the gardens. The little girl's nurse sat near to my nurse and I began to play with the dog. I was too shy to speak to the girl or even 15
look at her properly. She had a blue velvet coat and little blue boots. I can see those blue boots very clearly. Perhaps that was all I let myself see of her in the first days. She was just a blurred thing near to where I was playing with the dog. I liked playing with the dog, that was real playing, but I wanted much more to play with the little girl, but she would go and 20
sit beside her nurse, though I heard her more than once being told that she might play with me if she wished.

Then she began to come near to me when I was petting the dog, and once when I was sitting on the grass with the dog lying beside me she came and sat down beside the dog too, and I asked her the dog's name. I 25
can still feel the warm smooth feeling of the dog's back on which I had put my hand and I can see her hand near to mine stroking the dog's ears, and now I can see her face as I first saw it clearly for the first

a round rosy rather shiny glowing face. She had short very fair ›nd a funny little cross mouth and I loved her. We talked a little bit then she asked me to play with her. I was an only child and I did ‹ know how one played with another child. I knew no games which ›uld be played except alone. I said I would play with her but did not ‹hen know what to do. She tried to teach me a game, but I was too foolish and too much loving to understand, and I think anyway it was a game needing more people. In the end we just played with the dog, running races with it and teasing it and trying to make it do tricks. Now I wanted every day to come to the public gardens to see the little girl and I was very very happy. I think I was happier in those days than I have ever been since in my whole life. Then one day I thought I would like to bring a present to the little girl and the dog, and I persuaded my parents to buy a little yellow bouncing ball for the dog to play with and for us to throw and for him to bring back. I was so impatient for the next morning, I could hardly wait to show my friend the yellow ball and to throw it for the little dog. Next morning then I went to the gardens, and there was the girl in her blue coat and her blue boots and the black and white dog frisking round about her. I showed her the yellow ball and I threw it for the dog and he went running after it and he caught it and it stuck in his throat and he choked and died.'

30 35 40 45

Authors

'Saki' (H H Munro) (1870-1916) was born in Burma. His mother died when he was young, and he was educated and brought up in England. He joined the military police in Burma in 1893, but left because of an injury and settled in London where he decided to earn his living by writing. In 1899 he published *The Rise of the Russian Empire,* but after this he concentrated on journalism and short story writing. His short stories, published under the pseudonym of 'Saki' (the derivation is unknown), are *Reginald* (1904), *Reginald in Russia* (1910), *The Chronicles of Clovis* (1911), *Beasts and Super-Beasts* (1914), *The Toys of Peace* (1919) and *The Square Egg* (1924). A convenient collection is *The Best of Saki,* chosen by the comic novelist Tom Sharpe (published by Picador, 1976). In 1914 he joined the army to fight in France, where he was killed in 1916.

His short stories which are often very funny and satirical, are usually distinguished by a macabre, 'black' streak. Many of the best involve the appearance of animals as a kind of agent of revenge upon man (see his excellent stories *Sredni Vashtar, Tobermory,* and *The Remoulding of Groby Lington*). The blackness of his stories can be compared to those of Roald Dahl (see *Lamb to the Slaughter,* Chapter 6).

Rasipuram Krishnaswami Narayan, who was born in 1906, is an Indian who writes in English. He was born in Madras and educated at Mysore. He was for a short time a teacher, then a journalist, and in 1935 published his first novel *Swami and Friends*. In this novel he created the imaginary small town of Malgudi, which is the setting of several subsequent novels, including *The Bachelor of Arts* (1937), *The English Teacher* (1945), *The Vendor of Sweets* (1967) and *The Painter of Signs* (1977). The characters in his novels face the problems of reconciling Indian traditions with attitudes they have inherited from the British during the days of the British Empire (India became independent in 1947). His short stories are to be found in the collections *An Astrologer's Day and Other Stories* (1947), *Lawley Road* (1956), *A Horse and Two Goats* (1970). *Malgudi Days* (1982) and *Under the Banyan Tree and Other Stories* (1985), from which this story is taken.

Although Narayan may be the same age as Nambi there is no sign of a reduction in his powers of story-telling.

Iris Murdoch, who was born in 1919, is one of England's best-known contemporary novelists. For a long time she lectured on philosophy at Oxford University, and has written many successful novels which are distinguished by their portrayal of romantic and sexual complications, usually among the educated middle classes.

2 Love in Vain

A DILL PICKLE
Katherine Mansfield

Before you read

This story begins with a couple meeting in a café.

'And then, after six years, she saw him again.'	The first sentence of the story.
'In the past when they had looked at each other like that they had felt such a boundless understanding between them . . .'	From the middle of the story.
'She had gone. He sat there, thunder-struck, astounded beyond words.'	One of the closing sentences.

1 a) What do you think is the relationship between the man and woman?
b) What might have happened during their meeting?

A Dill Pickle

And then, after six years, she saw him again. He was seated at one of those little bamboo tables decorated with a Japanese vase of paper daffodils. There was a tall plate of fruit in front of him, and very carefully, in a way she recognized immediately as his 'special' way, he was peeling an orange. 5

He must have felt that shock of recognition in her for he looked up and met her eyes. Incredible! He didn't know her! She smiled; he frowned. She came towards him. He closed his eyes an instant, but opening them his face lit up as though he had struck a match in a dark room. He laid down the orange and pushed back his chair, and she took 10 her little warm hand out of her muff and gave it to him.

'Vera!' he exclaimed. 'How strange. Really, for a moment I didn't know you. Won't you sit down? You've had lunch? Won't you have some coffee?'

She hesitated, but of course she meant to. 15

'Yes, I'd like some coffee.' And she sat down opposite him.

'You've changed. You've changed very much,' he said, staring at her with that eager, lighted look. 'You look so well. I've never seen you look so well before.'

'Really?' She raised her veil and unbuttoned her high fur collar. 'I don't feel very well. I can't bear this weather, you know.' 20

'Ah, no. You hate the cold. . . .'

'Loathe it.' She shuddered. 'And the worst of it is that the older one grows . . .'

He interrupted her. 'Excuse me,' and tapped on the table for the waitress. 'Please bring some coffee and cream.' To her: 'You are sure you won't eat anything? Some fruit, perhaps. The fruit here is very good.' 25

'No, thanks. Nothing.'

'Then that's settled.' And smiling just a hint too broadly he took up the orange again. 'You were saying – the older one grows –' 30

'The colder,' she laughed. But she was thinking how well she remembered that trick of his – the trick of interrupting her – and of how it used to exasperate her six years ago. She used to feel then as though he, quite suddenly, in the middle of what she was saying, put his hand over her lips, turned from her, attended to something different, and then took his hand away, and with just the same slightly too broad smile, gave her his attention again. . . . Now we are ready. That is settled. 35

'The colder!' He echoed her words, laughing too. 'Ah, ah. You still say the same things. And there is another thing about you that is not changed at all – your beautiful voice – your beautiful way of speaking.' Now he was very grave; he leaned towards her, and she smelled the warm, stinging scent of the orange peel. 'You have only to say one word and I would know your voice among all other voices. I don't know what it is – I've often wondered – that makes your voice such a – haunting memory . . . Do you remember that first afternoon we spent together at Kew Gardens? You were so surprised because I did not know the names of any flowers. I am still just as ignorant for all your telling me. But whenever it is very fine and warm, and I see some bright colours – it's awfully strange – I hear your voice saying: "Geranium, marigold, and verbena." And I feel those three words are all I recall of some forgotten, heavenly language. . . . You remember that afternoon?' 40 45 50

What do you think her memories will be like – as romantic as his, or in any way different?

'Oh, yes, very well.' She drew a long, soft breath, as though the paper daffodils between them were almost too sweet to bear. Yet, what had remained in her mind of that particular afternoon was an absurd scene over the tea table. A great many people taking tea in a Chinese pagoda, and he behaving like a maniac about the wasps – waving them away, flapping at them with his straw hat, serious and infuriated out of all proportion to the occasion. How delighted the sniggering tea drinkers had been. And how she had suffered. 55 60

But now, as he spoke, that memory faded. His was the truer. Yes, it had been a wonderful afternoon, full of geranium and marigold and verbena, and – warm sunshine. Her thoughts lingered over the last two words as though she sang them.

In the warmth, as it were, another memory unfolded. She saw herself sitting on a lawn. He lay beside her, and suddenly, after a long silence, he rolled over and put his head in her lap.

'I wish,' he said in a low, troubled voice, 'I wish that I had taken poison and were about to die – here now!'

At that moment a little girl in a white dress, holding a long, dripping water lily, dodged from behind a bush, stared at them, and dodged back again. But he did not see. She leaned over him.

'Ah, why do you say that? I could not say that.'

But he gave a kind of soft moan, and taking her hand he held it to his cheek.

'Because I know I am going to love you too much – far too much. And I shall suffer so terribly, Vera, because you never, never will love me.'

He was certainly far better looking now than he had been then. He had lost all that dreamy vagueness and indecision. Now he had the air of a man who has found his place in life, and fills it with a confidence and an assurance which was, to say the least, impressive. He must have made money, too. His clothes were admirable, and at that moment he pulled a Russian cigarette case out of his pocket.

'Won't you smoke?'

'Yes, I will.' She hovered over them. 'They look very good.'

'I think they are. I get them made for me by a little man in St James's Street. I don't smoke very much. I'm not like you – but when I do, they must be delicious, very fresh cigarettes. Smoking isn't a habit with me; it's a luxury – like perfume. Are you still so fond of perfumes? Ah, when I was in Russia . . .'

She broke in: 'You've really been to Russia?'

'Oh, yes. I was there for over a year. Have you forgotten how we used to talk of going there?'

'No, I've not forgotten.'

He gave a strange half laugh and leaned back in his chair.

'Isn't it curious? I have really carried out all those journeys that we planned. Yes, I have been to all those places that we talked of, and stayed in them long enough to – as you used to say, "air oneself" in them. In fact, I have spent the last three years of my life travelling all the time. Spain, Corsica, Siberia, Russia, Egypt. The only country left is China, and I mean to go there, too, when the war is over.'

How do you think she will react to the news that he has 'carried out all those journeys that we planned'?

As he spoke, so lightly, tapping the end of his cigarette against the ash-tray, she felt the strange beast that had slumbered so long within her bosom stir, stretch itself, yawn, prick up its ears, and suddenly bound to its feet, and fix its longing, hungry stare upon those far away places. But all she said was, smiling gently: 'How I envy you.'

He accepted that. 'It has been,' he said, 'very wonderful – especially Russia. Russia was all that we had imagined, and far, far more. I even spent some days on a river boat on the Volga. Do you remember that boatman's song that you used to play?' 110

'Yes.' It began to play in her mind as she spoke.

'Do you ever play it now?'

'No, I've no piano.'

He was amazed at that. 'But what has become of your beautiful piano?' 115

She made a little grimace. 'Sold. Ages ago.'

'But you were so fond of music,' he wondered.

'I've no time for it now,' said she.

He let it go at that. 'That river life,' he went on, 'is something quite special. After a day or two you cannot realize that you have ever known 120 another. And it is not necessary to know the language – the life of the boat creates a bond between you and the people that's more than sufficient. You eat with them, pass the day with them, and in the evening there is that endless singing.'

She shivered, hearing the boatman's song break out again loud and 125 tragic, and seeing the boat floating on the darkening river with melancholy trees on either side . . . 'Yes, I should like that,' said she, stroking her muff.

'You'd like almost everything about Russian life,' he said warmly. 'It's so informal, so impulsive, so free without question. And then the 130 peasants are so splendid. They are such human beings – yes, that is it. Even the man who drives your carriage has – has some real part in what is happening. I remember the evening a party of us, two friends of mine and the wife of one of them, went for a picnic by the Black Sea. We took supper and champagne and ate and drank on the grass. And while we 135 were eating the coachman came up. "Have a dill pickle," he said. He wanted to share with us. That seemed to me so right, so – you know what I mean?'

And she seemed at that moment to be sitting on the grass beside the mysteriously Black Sea, black as velvet, and rippling against the banks 140 in silent, velvet waves. She saw the carriage drawn up to one side of the road, and the little group on the grass, their faces and hands white in the moonlight. She saw the pale dress of the woman outspread and her folded parasol, lying on the grass like a huge pearl crochet hook. Apart from them, with his supper in a cloth on his knees, sat the coachman. 145 'Have a dill pickle,' said he, and although she was not certain what a dill pickle was, she saw the greenish glass jar with a red chili like a parrot's beak glimmering through. She sucked in her cheeks; the dill pickle was terribly sour. . . .

'Yes, I know perfectly what you mean,' she said. 150

In the pause that followed they looked at each other. In the past when they had looked at each other like that they had felt such a boundless understanding between them that their souls had, as it were, put their arms round each other and dropped into the same sea, content to be drowned, like mournful lovers. But now, the surprising thing was that it was he who held back. He who said: 155

'What a marvellous listener you are. When you look at me with those wild eyes I feel that I could tell you things that I would never breathe to another human being.'

Was there just a hint of mockery in his voice or was it her fancy? She could not be sure. 160

How is she beginning to feel now?

'Before I met you,' he said, 'I had never spoken of myself to anybody. How well I remember one night, the night that I brought you the little Christmas tree, telling you all about my childhood. And of how I was so miserable that I ran away and lived under a cart in our yard for two days without being discovered. And you listened, and your eyes shone, and I felt that you had even made the little Christmas tree listen too, as in a fairy story.' 165

But of that evening she had remembered a little pot of caviare. It had cost seven and sixpence. He could not get over it. Think of it – a tiny jar like that costing seven and sixpence. While she ate it he watched her, delighted and shocked. 170

'No, really, that is eating money. You could not get seven shillings into a little pot that size. Only think of the profit they must make. . . .' And he had begun some immensely complicated calculations. . . . But now good-bye to the caviare. The Christmas tree was on the table, and the little boy lay under the cart with his head pillowed on the yard dog. 175

'The dog was called Bosun,' she cried delightedly.

But he did not follow. 'Which dog? Had you a dog? I don't remember a dog at all.' 180

'No, no. I meant the yard dog when you were a little boy.' He laughed and snapped the cigarette case to.

'Was he? Do you know I had forgotten that. It seems such ages ago. I cannot believe that it is only six years. After I had recognized you today – I had to take such a leap – I had to take a leap over my whole life to get back to that time. I was such a kid then.' He drummed on the table. 'I've often thought how I must have bored you. And now I understand so perfectly why you wrote to me as you did – although at the time that letter nearly finished my life. I found it again the other day, and I couldn't help laughing as I read it. It was so clever – such a true picture of me.' He glanced up. 'You're not going?' 185 190

She had buttoned her collar again and drawn down her veil.

'Yes, I am afraid I must,' she said, and managed a smile. Now she knew that he had been mocking.

'Ah, no, please,' he pleaded. 'Don't go just for a moment,' and he caught up one of her gloves from the table and clutched at it as if that would hold her. 'I see so few people to talk to nowadays, that I have turned into a sort of barbarian,' he said. 'Have I said something to hurt you?' 195

'Not a bit,' she lied. But as she watched him draw her glove through his fingers, gently, gently, her anger really did die down, and besides, at the moment he looked more like himself of six years ago. . . . 200

How do you think the story will develop?

'What I really wanted then,' he said softly, 'was to be a sort of carpet – to make myself into a sort of carpet for you to walk on so that you need not be hurt by the sharp stones and the mud that you hated so. It was nothing more positive than that – nothing more selfish. Only I did desire, eventually, to turn into a magic carpet and carry you away to all those lands you longed to see.' 205

As he spoke she lifted her head as though she drank something; the strange beast in her bosom began to purr. . . . 210

'I felt that you were more lonely than anybody else in the world,' he went on, 'and yet, perhaps, that you were the only person in the world who was really, truly alive. Born out of your time,' he murmured, stroking the glove, 'fated.'

Ah, God! What had she done! How had she dared to throw away her happiness like this. This was the only man who had ever understood her. Was it too late? Could it be too late? *She* was that glove that he held in his fingers. . . . 215

'And then the fact that you had no friends and never had made friends with people. How I understood that, for neither had I. Is it just the same now?' 220

'Yes,' she breathed. 'Just the same. I am as alone as ever.'

'So am I,' he laughed gently, 'just the same.'

Suddenly with a quick gesture he handed her back the glove and scraped his chair on the floor. 'But what seemed to me so mysterious then is perfectly plain to me now. And to you, too, of course. . . . It simply was that we were such egoists, so self-engrossed, so wrapped up in ourselves that we hadn't a corner in our hearts for anybody else. Do you know,' he cried, naïve and hearty, and dreadfully like another side of that old self again, 'I began studying a Mind System when I was in Russia, and I found that we were not peculiar at all. It's quite a well-known form of . . .' 225 230

She had gone. He sat there, thunder-struck, astounded beyond words. . . . And then he asked the waitress for his bill.

'But the cream has not been touched,' he said. 'Please do not charge me for it.' 235

See Glossary section at the back of the book for vocabulary.

First reaction

2 **a)** Who do you think has been moved more by this meeting, the man or the woman?

b) Why does the woman leave so suddenly?

Close reading

Interpreting characters' feelings
An interesting effect is created by the difference between what the characters say and what they feel. In a sense, the reader has to do a lot of 'reading between the lines' (interpreting) to decide what is going on, and to appreciate the story fully.

3 The woman

The woman says very little during the meeting, yet the reader gets the strong impression that she is very involved emotionally: we are often shown the woman's thoughts, and sometimes the reporting verb gives us an idea of how she feels. Also, perhaps the fact that she speaks so little, and is so restrained in what she says, is evidence that she feels deeply.

In this exercise, try to put into your own words what she is feeling when she speaks. The first four have been done as examples, but you can change them if you have different ideas. Then continue by writing your own interpretations.

What she says	*What she is feeling*
Yes, I'd like some coffee. (line 16)	After all these years! I'd love to speak to him.
Oh, yes, very well. (line 53)	He's right – that afternoon was more romantic than I had thought. Perhaps I didn't appreciate this love affair enough.
You've really been to Russia? . . . No, I've not forgotten. (lines 91-4)	I thought we were just dreaming when we talked about going on those journeys.
How I envy you. (line 106)	I had forgotten all those ambitions I used to have. I wonder if I have missed an opportunity in life?
Yes, I should like that. (line 127)	______________________ ______________________
Yes, I know perfectly what you mean. (line 150)	______________________ ______________________
Yes, I'm afraid I must. (line 193)	______________________ ______________________
Not a bit. (line 200)	______________________ ______________________

Yes, just the same. I am as alone as ever. (line 222) ______________________________

____

4 The man

The man, on the other hand, speaks a lot during the meeting, yet what does the reader think of his emotional involvement? Choose the interpretation that you agree with, or write one of your own.

What he says	*How the reader judges it*
Really, for a moment I didn't know you. (lines 12-13)	**a)** genuine surprise **b)** rather a cold greeting **c)** a hurtful thing to say **d)** understandably, his emotions are confused – he doesn't know what to say
You have only to say one word and I would know your voice among all other voices. (lines 43-4)	**a)** a sincere emotion beautifully expressed **b)** this is not really deep emotion: he just likes to speak in this 'poetic' way **c)** this is perhaps true, but this exaggerated expression makes me rather suspicious of him **d)** something he has always wanted to say, but only now does he have the courage
I get them made for me . . . it's a luxury – like perfume. (lines 86-9)	**a)** how pretentious! **b)** how refined! **c)** how sensual! **d)** how ridiculous!
I have really carried out all those journeys that we planned. (lines 96-7)	**a)** an insensitive thing to say **b)** he's more interested in what he has done than what she has done **c)** he's showing her how important she was for his development **d)** an interesting topic of conversation
He let it go at that. That river life, he went on . . . (line 119)	**a)** diplomatic: he's avoiding a subject that seems painful to her **b)** understandable: he's eager to tell her this interesting story **c)** selfish: he's not interested in what has happened to her

d) insensitive: why doesn't he find out why she has sold the piano and try to console her?

And then the peasants are so splendid. They are such human beings – yes, that is it. (lines 130-1)

____
____
____

What a marvellous listener you are . . . I would never breathe to another human being. (lines 157-9)

____
____
____

Was he? Do you know I had forgotten that. It seems such ages ago. (line 183)

____
____
____

I found it again the other day and I couldn't help laughing as I read it. (lines 189-90)

____
____
____

But the cream has not been touched. Please do not charge me for it. (lines 235-6)

____
____
____

And, finally, what he *doesn't* say: He sat there, thunder-struck, astounded beyond words. (lines 233-4)

a) the poor man how he must be suffering!
b) poetic justice! Finally, after so much talking, he finds himself at a loss for words!
c) this is ironic exaggeration: his loss of speech lasts for a few seconds only
d) Your interpretation: ________

____
____

5 Compare how each character has been affected by this meeting. Do you think, as the woman thinks, that the man has been mocking her?

Language practice

Describing past habits and changes – *used to; still; not any more/no longer*

'. . . she remembered that trick of his – the trick of interrupting her – and of how it used to exasperate her six years ago.' (lines 32-4)

Part of the effect of this story comes from the observation of how people change or don't change with the passing of time, and of how they remember the past.

6 Answer the following questions with 'used to'.

a) What is suggested in the story about the man at the time of their love affair? Consider:
- **i)** his character (lines 78-81; 54-9)
  e.g. He used to be vague and indecisive. (lines 78-9)
  He used to overreact to situations and/or He didn't use to have much social grace. (lines 54-9)
- **ii)** his financial situation (lines 81-2; 169-75)
- **iii)** his feelings towards Vera (lines 68-77; 162-8).

b) What is suggested in the story about the woman at the time of their love affair? Consider:
- **i)** her character (lines 219-22)
- **ii)** her ambitions; what she wanted from life (lines 102-6)
- **iii)** her feelings towards the man (lines 151-5).

c) Look at lines 183-end where the man gives *his* analysis of their love affair.
- **i)** What does the man think he used to be like – what is his impression of his past self? (lines 183-91)
- **ii)** What does the man think she used to be like? (lines 211-14)
- **iii)** How does he criticise both himself and her? (lines 225-32)

7 Write sentences with *still* and *not . . . any more/no longer.*

a)
- **i)** He/peel oranges/a particular way
- **ii)** He/interrupt people
- **iii)** She/have/beautiful voice
- **iv)** He/know the names/flowers
- **v)** He/be poor
- **vi)** He/remember the name/his dog

b) **i)** Do you think she still loves him? Does he still love her?
ii) What is your interpretation of lines 109-18? Doesn't she like music any more? If not, why not? Or is the explanation that she is no longer well-off, and has had to sell her piano?

Vocabulary

Explaining the effect of similes and metaphors

8 A **simile** is an *explicit* comparison between object A and another object B, in the form 'A is like B' or 'A is as . . . (adjective) as B'. There must be some similarity or point of comparison between A and B. For example:

O, my Love's like a red red rose
That's newly sprung in June:

Robert Burns (1759-96)

Object A is the lover, 'my Love', Object B is the 'red red rose'. The point of comparison is beauty and freshness. Notice that in this simile we do not consider other qualities of a rose – it has thorns, it dies every year (although we may consider them in other similes).

9 A **metaphor** is an *implicit* comparison between object A and another object B. The words that make the explicit comparison – *like, as* or *as if/as though* – are not there; a metaphor takes the form 'A is B'. A metaphor can be composed of nouns, adjectives and verbs. As with a simile, there must be some similarity or point of comparison between A and B.

'My days are in the yellow leaf;
The flowers and fruits of love are gone.'

Lord Byron (1788-1824)

Here, age is compared to the yellow leaves of autumn, and love is compared to fruit and flowers.

10 Consider these extracts from the story:

a) 'As he spoke, so lightly, tapping the end of his cigarette against the ash-tray, she felt the strange beast that had slumbered so long within her bosom stir, stretch itself, yawn, prick up its ears, and suddenly bound to its feet and fix its long hungry stare upon those far away places.' (lines 102-5).

There is a metaphor here composed of: Object A – what the woman wants from life; Object B – a strange beast.

b) 'As he spoke she lifted her head as though she drank something . . .' (line 209)

This is a simile, composed of: Object A – the movement of her head while the man speaks; Object B – drinking.

Look at how an interpretation of these extracts might be written:

In these extracts, what she wants from life is compared to a strange beast, a magnificent animal that even she doesn't understand well. The first extract contains a metaphor which suggests that what she wants from life has been for some time suppressed, but that it is something that cannot be tamed or controlled permanently. It is something that needs to have its appetite satisfied. In the second extract the simile 'she lifted her head as though she drank something' gives the idea that she enjoys, perhaps needs, what the man says.

Do you agree with this interpretation? Is there anything you would add or take away?

11 Write an interpretation of the following extract similar to the interpretation in 10 above.

'What I really wanted then, . . . was to be a sort of carpet – to make myself into a sort of carpet for you to walk on so that you need not be hurt by the sharp stones and the mud that you hated so . . . Only I did desire, eventually, to turn into a magic carpet and carry you away to all those lands you longed to see.' (lines 203-8)

12 Write interpretations for these extracts.

a) 'In the past when they had looked at each other like that they had felt such a boundless understanding between them that their souls had, as it were, put their arms round each other and dropped into the same sea, content to be drowned, like mournful lovers'. (lines 151-5)

b) '*She* was that glove that he held in his fingers . . .' (lines 217-18)

Extension

13 Discussion

Make some notes about what you used to be like in the past (you choose how long ago). In what ways have you changed, and in what ways haven't you changed? Instead of yourself, you can discuss the changes in a friend, relative or partner (boyfriend/girlfriend, wife/husband).

'His were the truer', the woman thinks, comparing her memories with the man's (line 61). Have you ever experienced this – comparing your memories with someone else's memories of the same event and finding them different?

Why did Katherine Mansfield choose the title *A Dill Pickle?* Do you think this title is in any way symbolic?

14 Composition

Write the letter Vera wrote to her lover (lines 187-91). Take into consideration her reasons for writing it, the tone and the content. (about 150 words)

Beyond the text

15 Nostalgia

'Strange, the potency of cheap music', a character remarks in the Noel Coward play *Private Lives* (1933). He is referring to the way that popular songs can often 'put their finger on' an emotion or mood, and describe it exactly. Look at this song by George and Ira Gershwin and fill in the blanks with a suitable word. As at the beginning of *A Dill Pickle,* it refers to the fact that even after a love affair has finished the particular habits of the lover remain in the memory.

(Note. Blank **(9)** is the only example of a past tense. The other verbs are in the present tense.)

They can't take that away from me

The way you (**1**) ________ your hat,
The way you sip your tea,
The (**2**) ________ of all that,
No, no, they can't take that away from me.

The way (**3**) ________ smile just beams,
The way you (**4**) ________ off key,
The way you (**5**) ________ my dreams,
No, no, they can't take that away from me.

We may never, never meet again
(**6**) ________ the bumpy road to (**7**) ________,
Still, I'll always, always keep the memory of

The way you (**8**) ________ your knife,
The way we (**9**) ________ till three,
The way you've changed my (**10**) ________,
No, no, they can't take that away from me.

Author

Katherine Mansfield (1888-1923) was born in Wellington, New Zealand and completed her education at Queen's College, London (1903-6). She returned to New Zealand to study music, but went back to London after two years. She married in 1909, but left her husband after a few days. In 1911 she met the critic and editor of Modernist literary magazines, John Middleton Murry, whom she married in 1918. In 1916 she discovered she had tuberculosis, of which she died in 1923.

She published several volumes of short stories in her lifetime, the most famous being *Bliss and other stories* (1920), from which *A Dill Pickle* is taken, and *The Garden Party and other stories* (1922). Her short stories, varying in length and tone, are thought by many critics to show the influence of the Russian short story writer, Chekhov.

3 Childhood Memories

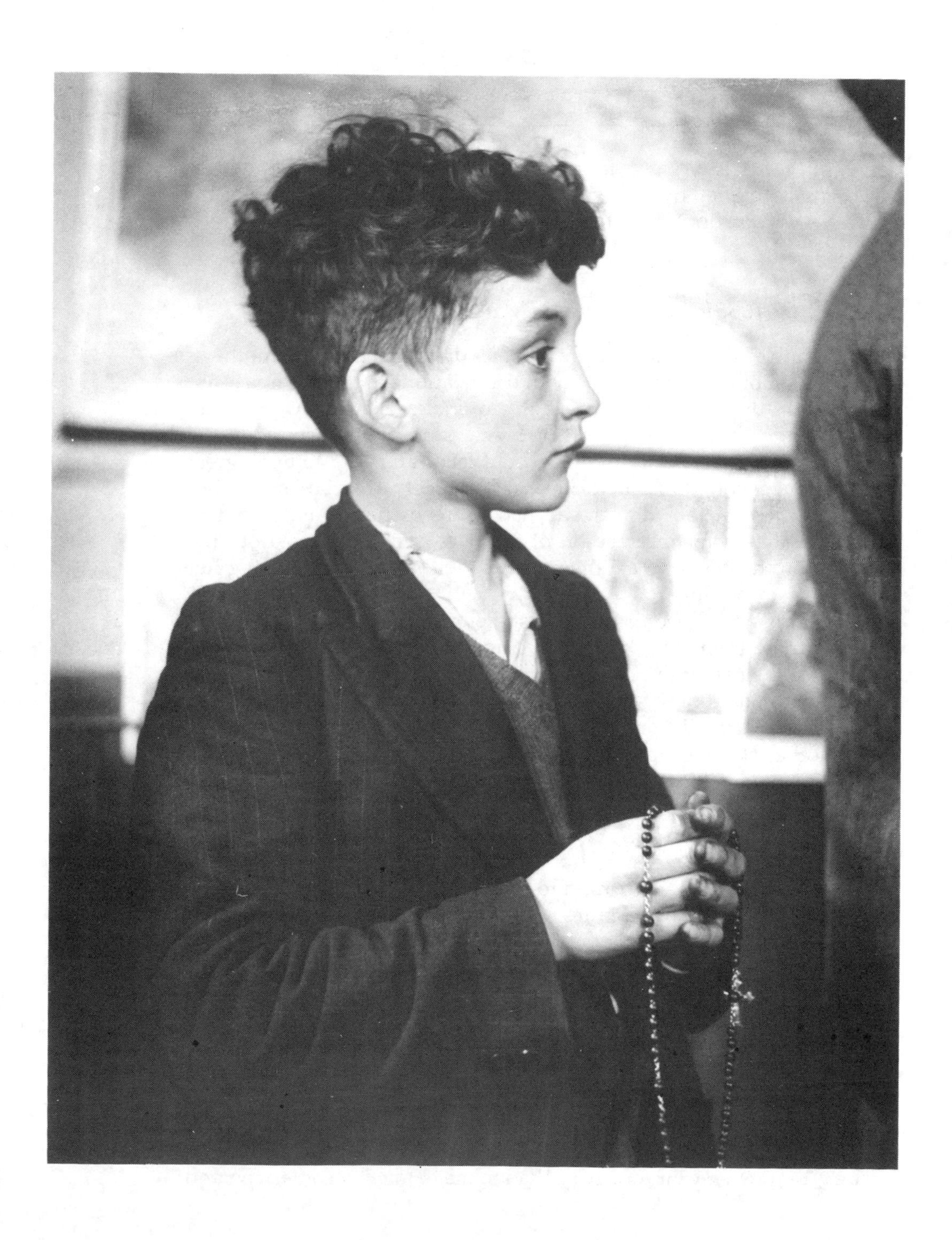

FIRST CONFESSION
Frank O'Connor

Before you read

1 Think back to your childhood. What things do you remember being frightened by? Did you ever have an experience where you were very anxious, but which finished with a great sense of relief?

First Confession

All the trouble began when my grandfather died and my grandmother – my father's mother – came to live with us. Relations in the one house are a strain at the best of times, but, to make matters worse, my grandmother was a real old country-woman and quite unsuited to the life in town. She had a fat, wrinkled old face, and, to Mother's great indignation, went round the house in bare feet – the boots had her crippled, she said. For dinner she had a jug of porter and a pot of potatoes with – sometimes – a bit of salt fish, and she poured out the potatoes on the table and ate them slowly, with great relish, using her fingers by way of a fork. 5 10

Now, girls are supposed to be fastidious, but I was the one who suffered most from this. Nora, my sister, just sucked up to the old woman for the penny she got every Friday out of the old-age pension, a thing I could not do. I was too honest, that was my trouble; and when I was playing with Bill Connell, the sergeant-major's son, and saw my grandmother steering up the path with the jug of porter sticking out from beneath her shawl, I was mortified. I made excuses not to let him come into the house, because I could never be sure what she would be up to when we went in. 15

When Mother was at work and my grandmother made the dinner I wouldn't touch it. Nora once tried to make me, but I hid under the table from her and took the bread-knife with me for protection. Nora let on to be very indignant (she wasn't, of course, but she knew Mother saw through her, so she sided with Gran) and came after me. I lashed out at her with the bread-knife, and after that she left me alone. I stayed there till Mother came in from work and made my dinner, but when Father came in later Nora said in a shocked voice: 'Oh, Dadda, do you know what Jackie did at dinner-time?' Then, of course, it all came out; Father gave me a flaking; Mother interfered, and for days after that he didn't speak to me and Mother barely spoke to Nora. And all because of that old woman! God knows, I was heart-scalded. 20 25 30

Then, to crown my misfortunes, I had to make my first confession and communion. It was an old woman called Ryan who prepared us for these. She was about the one age with Gran; she was well-to-do, lived in a big house on Montenotte, wore a black cloak and bonnet, and came every day to school at three o'clock when we should have been going home, and talked to us of hell. She may have mentioned the other place as well, but that could only have been by accident, for hell had the first place in her heart.

What do you think Mrs Ryan will say about hell?

She lit a candle, took out a new half-crown, and offered it to the first boy who would hold one finger – only one finger! – in the flame for five minutes by the school clock. Being always very ambitious I was tempted to volunteer, but I thought it might look greedy. Then she asked were we afraid of holding one finger – only one finger! – in a little candle flame for five minutes and not afraid of burning all over in roasting hot furnaces for all eternity. 'All eternity! Just think of that! A whole lifetime goes by and it's nothing, not even a drop in the ocean of your sufferings.' The woman was really interesting about hell, but my attention was all fixed on the half-crown. At the end of the lesson she put it back in her purse. It was a great disappointment; a religious woman like that, you wouldn't think she'd bother about a thing like a half-crown.

Another day she said she knew a priest who woke one night to find a fellow he didn't recognize leaning over the end of his bed. The priest was a bit frightened – naturally enough – but he asked the fellow what he wanted, and the fellow said in a deep, husky voice that he wanted to go to confession. The priest said it was an awkward time and wouldn't it do in the morning, but the fellow said that last time he went to confession, there was one sin he kept back, being ashamed to mention it, and now it was always on his mind. Then the priest knew it was a bad case, because the fellow was after making a bad confession and committing a mortal sin. He got up to dress, and just then the cock crew in the yard outside, and – lo and behold! – when the priest looked round there was no sign of the fellow, only a smell of burning timber, and when the priest looked at his bed didn't he see the print of two hands burned in it! That was because the fellow had made a bad confession. This story made a shocking impression on me.

But the worst of all was when she showed us how to examine our conscience. Did we take the name of the Lord, our God, in vain? Did we honour our father and our mother? (I asked her did this include grandmothers and she said it did.) Did we love our neighbours as ourselves? Did we covet our neighbour's goods? (I thought of the way I felt about the penny that Nora got every Friday.) I decided that, between one thing and another, I must have broken the whole ten commandments, all on account of that old woman, and so far as I could see, so long as she remained in the house I had no hope of ever doing anything else.

I was scared to death of confession. The day the whole class went I let on to have a toothache, hoping my absence wouldn't be noticed; but at three o'clock, just as I was feeling safe, along comes a chap with a message from Mrs Ryan that I was to go to confession myself on Saturday and be at the chapel for communion with the rest. To make it worse, Mother couldn't come with me and sent Nora instead. 80

Now, that girl had ways of tormenting me that Mother never knew of. She held my hand as we went down the hill, smiling sadly and saying how sorry she was for me, as if she were bringing me to the hospital for an operation. 85

Before you read on, think briefly of 'the ways of tormenting him' that Nora might use.

'Oh, God, help us!' she moaned. 'Isn't it a terrible pity you weren't a good boy? Oh Jackie, my heart bleeds for you! How will you ever think of all your sins? Don't forget you have to tell him about the time you kicked Gran on the shin.'

'Lemme go!' I said, trying to drag myself free of her. 'I don't want to go to confession at all.' 90

'But sure, you'll have to go to confession, Jackie,' she replied in the same regretful tone. 'Sure, if you didn't, the parish priest would be up to the house, looking for you. 'Tisn't, God knows, that I'm not sorry for you. Do you remember the time you tried to kill me with the bread-knife under the table? And the language you used to me? I don't know what he'll do with you at all, Jackie. He might have to send you up to the bishop.' 95

I remember thinking bitterly that she didn't know the half of what I had to tell – if I told it. I knew I couldn't tell it, and understood perfectly why the fellow in Mrs Ryan's story made a bad confession; it seemed to me a great shame that people wouldn't stop criticizing him. I remember that steep hill down to the church, and the sunlit hillsides beyond the valley of the river, which I saw in the gaps between the houses like Adam's last glimpse of Paradise. 100

Then, when she had manoeuvred me down the long flight of steps to the chapel yard, Nora suddenly changed her tone. She became the raging malicious devil she really was. 105

'There you are!' she said with a yelp of triumph, hurling me through the church door. 'And I hope he'll give you the penitential psalms, you dirty little caffler.' 110

I knew then I was lost, given up to eternal justice. The door with the coloured-glass panels swung shut behind me, the sunlight went out and gave place to deep shadow, and the wind whistled outside so that the silence within seemed to crackle like ice under my feet. Nora sat in front of me by the confession box. There were a couple of old women ahead of her, and then a miserable-looking poor devil came and wedged me in at the other side, so that I couldn't escape even if I had the courage. He joined his hands and rolled his eyes in the direction of the roof, muttering aspirations in an anguished tone, and I wondered had he a 115 grandmother too. Only a grandmother could account for a fellow behaving in that heart-broken way, but he was better off than I, for he at least could go and confess his sins; while I would make a bad confession and then die in the night and be continually coming back and burning people's furniture. 120

Nora's turn came, and I heard the sound of something slamming, and then her voice as if butter wouldn't melt in her mouth, and then another slam, and out she came. God, the hypocrisy of women! Her eyes were lowered, her head was bowed, and her hands were joined very low down on her stomach, and she walked up the aisle to the side altar looking like a saint. You never saw such an exhibition of devotion; and I remembered the devilish malice with which she had tormented me all the way from our door, and wondered were all religious people like that, really. It was my turn now. With the fear of damnation in my soul I went in, and the confessional door closed of itself behind me. 125 130

What do you think is going to happen now?

It was pitch-dark and I couldn't see priest or anything else. Then I really began to be frightened. In the darkness it was a matter between God and me, and He had all the odds. He knew what my intentions were before I even started; I had no chance. All I had ever been told about confession got mixed up in my mind, and I knelt to one wall and said: 'Bless me, father, for I have sinned; this is my first confession.' I waited for a few minutes, but nothing happened, so I tried it on the other wall. Nothing happened there either. He had me spotted all right. 135 140

It must have been then that I noticed the shelf at about one height with my head. It was really a place for grown-up people to rest their elbows, but in my distracted state I thought it was probably the place you were supposed to kneel. Of course, it was on the high side and not very deep, but I was always good at climbing and managed to get up all right. Staying up was the trouble. There was room only for my knees, and nothing you could get a grip on but a sort of wooden moulding a bit above it. I held on to the moulding and repeated the words a little louder, and this time something happened all right. A slide was slammed back; a little light entered the box, and a man's voice said: 'Who's there?' 145 150

''Tis me, father,' I said for fear he mightn't see me and go away again. I couldn't see him at all. The place the voice came from was under the moulding, about level with my knees, so I took a good grip of the moulding and swung myself down till I saw the astonished face of a young priest looking up at me. He had to put his head on one side to see me, and I had to put mine on one side to see him, so we were more or less talking to one another upside-down. It struck me as a queer way of hearing confessions, but I didn't feel it my place to criticize. 155 160

'Bless me, father, for I have sinned; this is my first confession,' I rattled off all in one breath, and swung myself down the least shade more to make it easier for him.

'What are you doing up there?' he shouted in an angry voice, and the strain the politeness was putting on my hold of the moulding, and the shock of being addressed in such an uncivil tone, were too much for me. I lost my grip, tumbled, and hit the door an unmerciful wallop before I found myself flat on my back in the middle of the aisle. The people who had been waiting stood up with their mouths open. The priest opened the door of the middle box and came out, pushing his biretta back from his forehead; he looked something terrible. Then Nora came scampering down the aisle. 165 170

'Oh, you dirty little caffler!' she said. 'I might have known you'd do it. I might have known you'd disgrace me. I can't leave you out of my sight for one minute.' 175

Before I could even get to my feet to defend myself she bent down and gave me a clip across the ear. This reminded me that I was so stunned I had even forgotten to cry, so that people might think I wasn't hurt at all, when in fact I was probably maimed for life. I gave a roar out of me. 180

Things are going disastrously. How do you think the priest will react?

'What's all this about?' the priest hissed, getting angrier than ever and pushing Nora off me. 'How dare you hit the child like that, you little vixen?'

'But I can't do my penance with him, father,' Nora cried, cocking an outraged eye up at him. 185

'Well, go and do it, or I'll give you some more to do,' he said, giving me a hand up. 'Was it coming to confession you were, my poor man?' he asked me.

''Twas, father,' said I with a sob.

'Oh,' he said respectfully, 'a big hefty fellow like you must have terrible sins. Is this your first?' 190

''Tis, father,' said I.

'Worse and worse,' he said gloomily. 'The crimes of a lifetime. I don't know if I will get rid of you at all today. You'd better wait now till I'm finished with these old ones. You can see by the looks of them they haven't much to tell.' 195

'I will, father,' I said with something approaching joy.

The relief of it was really enormous. Nora stuck out her tongue at me from behind his back, but I couldn't even be bothered retorting. I knew from the very moment that man opened his mouth that he was intelligent above the ordinary. When I had time to think, I saw how right I was. It only stood to reason that a fellow confessing after seven years would have more to tell than people that went every week. The crimes of a lifetime, exactly as he said. It was only what he expected, and the rest was the cackle of old women and girls with their talk of hell, the bishop, and the penitential psalms. That was all they knew. I started to make my examination of conscience, and barring the one bad business of my grandmother it didn't seem so bad. 200 205

The next time, the priest steered me into the confession box himself and left the shutter back the way I could see him get in and sit down at the further side of the grille from me. 210

'Well, now,' he said, 'what do they call you?'

'Jackie, father,' said I.

'And what's a-trouble to you, Jackie?'

'Father,' I said, feeling I might as well get it over while I had him in good humour, 'I had it all arranged to kill my grandmother.' 215

What do you think the priest will say to this?

He seemed a bit shaken by that, all right, because he said nothing for quite a while.

'My goodness,' he said at last, 'that'd be a shocking thing to do. What put that into your head?' 220

'Father,' I said, feeling very sorry for myself, 'she's an awful woman.'

'Is she?' he asked. 'What way is she awful?'

'She takes porter, father,' I said, knowing well from the way Mother talked of it that this was a mortal sin, and hoping it would make the priest take a more favourable view of my case. 225

'Oh, my!' he said, and I could see he was impressed.

'And snuff, father,' said I.

'That's a bad case, sure enough, Jackie,' he said.

'And she goes round in her bare feet, father,' I went on in a rush of self-pity, 'and she know I don't like her, and she gives pennies to Nora and none to me, and my da sides with her and flakes me, and one night I was so heart-scalded I made up my mind I'd have to kill her.' 230

'And what would you do with the body?' he asked with great interest.

'I was thinking I could chop that up and carry it away in a barrow I have,' I said. 235

'Begor, Jackie,' he said, 'do you know you're a terrible child?'

'I know, father,' I said, for I was just thinking the same thing myself. 'I tried to kill Nora too with a bread-knife under the table, only I missed her.'

'Is that the little girl that was beating you just now?' he asked. 240

''Tis, father.'

'Someone will go for her with a bread-knife one day, and he won't miss her,' he said rather cryptically. 'You must have great courage. Between ourselves, there's a lot of people I'd like to do the same to but I'd never have the nerve. Hanging is an awful death.' 245

'Is it, father?' I asked with the deepest interest – I was always very keen on hanging. 'Did you ever see a fellow hanged?'

'Dozens of them,' he said solemnly. 'And they all died roaring.'

'Jay!' I said.

'Oh, a horrible death!' he said with great satisfaction. 'Lots of the fellows I saw killed their grandmothers too, but they all said 'twas never worth it.' 250

He had me there for a full ten minutes talking, and then walked out the chapel yard with me. I was genuinely sorry to part with him, because he was the most entertaining character I'd ever met in the religious line. Outside, after the shadow of the church, the sunlight was like the roaring of waves on a beach; it dazzled me; and when the frozen silence melted and I heard the screech of trams on the road my heart soared. I knew now I wouldn't die in the night and come back, leaving marks on my mother's furniture. It would be a great worry to her, and the poor soul had enough.

Jackie is now going to walk home with Nora. How do you think she is going to react to what has happened?

Nora was sitting on the railing, waiting for me, and she put on a very sour puss when she saw the priest with me. She was mad jealous because a priest had never come out of the church with her.

'Well,' she asked coldly, after he left me, 'what did he give you?'

'Three Hail Marys,' I said.

'Three Hail Marys,' she repeated incredulously. 'You mustn't have told him anything.'

'I told him everything,' I said confidently.

'About Gran and all?'

'About Gran and all.'

(All she wanted was to be able to go home and say I'd made a bad confession.)

'Did you tell him you went for me with the bread-knife?' she asked with a frown.

'I did to be sure.'

'And he only gave you three Hail Marys?'

'That's all.'

She slowly got down from the railing with a baffled air. Clearly, this was beyond her. As we mounted the steps back to the main road she looked at me suspiciously.

'What are you sucking?' she asked.

'Bullseyes.'

'Was it the priest gave them to you?'

''Twas.'

'Lord God,' she wailed bitterly, 'some people have all the luck! 'Tis no advantage to anybody trying to be good. I might just as well be a sinner like you.'

See Glossary section at the back of the book for vocabulary.

First reaction

2 ''Tis no advantage to anybody trying to be good. I might just as well be a sinner like you.'

This is Nora's comment on the events of the story, an interpretation from her point of view. O'Connor leaves the last word with her, giving the reader the satisfaction of seeing the real 'villain' of the story frustrated and defeated.

Write some other comments on the events of the story from other points of view. What comments might be made by:

a) the priest to a friend later in the day?
b) Nora and Jackie's mother when they get home and Nora starts complaining?
c) Jackie, as an adult looking back on this childhood experience?

Close reading

Discovering point of view and irony

3 Compare these sentences in lines 256-261 carefully.

a) 'Outside, after the shadow of the church, the sunlight was like the roaring of waves on a beach; it dazzled me; and when the frozen silence melted and I heard the screech of trams on the road my heart soared.
b) I knew now I wouldn't die in the night and come back, leaving marks on my mother's furniture.
c) It would be a great worry to her, and the poor soul had enough.'

All three sentences are narrated in the first person: 'I' and 'me'. In the first, the emotion – relief – is conveyed in sophisticated language: notice the simile 'the sunlight was like the roaring of waves on a beach' and the metaphor 'the frozen silence melted,' which build up the imagery of light after darkness, heat after cold and sound after silence that mirrors the change in the boy's mood from fear to relief.

The second and third sentences also describe Jackie's relief, but notice the naïvety of the thoughts expressed and the simple language: Jackie believes that a bad confession will make you burst into flames, and he is almost more relieved about his mother's furniture than about the salvation of his soul!

The moments are described from different *points of view*. The first sentence is an impression of the moment by the adult Jackie looking back into the past, while the second and third sentences are an impression of the same moment as it is felt by the young Jackie at the time of the story.

A writer can describe the events and characters in a story from different points of view; that is, the writer chooses a narrator who interprets the events of the story and conveys this interpretation to the reader. It is often interesting, when reading fiction, to ask the question 'Who is telling me this?' As we see in the example above, a writer can describe the same event from different points of view, giving the reader more than one interpretation and making the reading experience richer.

4 Who is the narrator in the following extracts from the story – the adult Jackie or the boy Jackie?

a) 'Relations in the one house are a strain at the best of times, but, to make matters worse, my grandmother was a real old country-woman and quite unsuited to the life in town.' (lines 2-5)

b) '. . . a religious woman like that, you wouldn't think she'd bother about a thing like a half-crown.' (lines 49-51)

c) 'I remember that steep hill down to the church, and the sunlit hillsides beyond the valley of the river, which I saw in the gaps between the houses like Adam's last glimpse of Paradise.' (lines 102-4)

d) 'Only a grandmother could account for a fellow behaving in that heart-broken way . . .' (lines 120-1)

e) '. . . people might think I wasn't hurt at all, when in fact I was probably maimed for life.' (lines 179-80)

O'Connor's use of different points of view contributes greatly to the comic effect of this story. The reader and the adult Jackie share the same point of view – that of an adult who can now look back with amusement at the exaggerated fears of childhood. The majority of the story is, however, narrated by the boy Jackie. . . . This kind of narrator is called a *fallible narrator*, a narrator who is a protagonist or main character in the story, but whose version of events is unreliable because it is influenced by personal interests, prejudice or, in this case, lack of experience. . . . This means O'Connor can use *irony*: the narrator tells us things in complete sincerity, believing them true, but the reader knows that it is not a realistic interpretation of events. In this case it is amusing, as we smile sympathetically at the innocence of childhood.

5 Consider the following example of irony.

'Oh,' he said respectfully, 'a big hefty fellow like you must have terrible sins.' (lines 190-1)

Here we appreciate the irony in:

a) what the priest says: he doesn't really think Jackie has committed terrible sins. The reader knows this, the adult Jackie knows this, but the boy Jackie doesn't.
b) the boy's interpretation of what the priest says: he *really* thinks the priest is speaking to him 'respectfully'.

Find other examples of these two kinds of irony in the conversation between Jackie and the priest (lines 190-252). You will find plenty of examples of both: for examples of type **b)** look at the extended comments of the young narrator, and the use of adverbs and adverbial phrases.

6 The reader also appreciates the irony in the way O'Connor shows us the world as judged by Jackie. Because of his limited experience of life, Jackie has a simple, ingenuous vision of the world. For example:

'Only a grandmother could account for a fellow behaving in that heart-broken way . . .' (lines 120-1)

Having a grandmother who drinks is the worst possible thing that Jackie can imagine, and he – for the reader, comically – measures everything against his own limited experience.

Find some other examples of Jackie's simple vision of the world in the scene between him and the priest (lines 190-261).

7 On the other hand, children have both the ability and the lack of social embarrassment to make penetrating observations about adults. For example, when Jackie talks about the embittered Mrs Ryan:

'She may have mentioned the other place as well, but that could only have been by accident, for hell had the first place in her heart.' (lines 36-8)

What do you think of the following comment? Do we immediately discount it as being simply a childish thought, or not?

'I remembered the devilish malice with which she had tormented me all the way from our door, and wondered were all religious people like that, really.' (lines 130-3)

Language practice

Creating different narrative effects – Direct and indirect speech

8 The choice of direct speech or indirect speech is important.

Direct speech

'Oh,' he said respectfully, 'a big hefty fellow like you must have terrible sins.' (lines 190-1)

The writer tells us exactly what the priest says (and so, in this case, we enjoy the priest's irony fully). The writer seems to disappear from the story, and leaves it to the reader to listen to the characters speaking, as if the reader were watching a play at the theatre, or a film. This often makes the story more vivid, and reveals character in a particularly life-like way. O'Connor, however, does not disappear completely. By the use of adverbs and adverbial phrases he also shows us the naïvety of the young narrator.

The character says: 'Oh, a big hefty fellow like you must have terrible sins.'
The narrator interprets: 'he said respectfully'.

Indirect speech

'I made excuses not to let him come into the house.' (lines 17-18)
Here, the exact words of the excuse are of no great interest, and so they are not given.

9 Experiment with the different effects produced by direct and indirect speech. Change the following examples of direct speech from the story into indirect speech. As you do so, ask yourself if you are simply making a grammatical change, or if you are changing the effect.

a) 'The crimes of a lifetime. I don't know if I will get rid of you at all today. You'd better wait now till I'm finished with these old ones. You can see by the looks of them they haven't much to tell.' (lines 193-6)

He said that mine were ________________ and that he didn't know if he ________________. He told me I'd ________________. He said I could ________________.

b) 'that'd be a shocking thing to do. What put that into your head?' (lines 219-20)

He said ________________ and asked me ________________.

c) 'That's a bad case, sure enough, Jackie' (line 228)

He agreed with me that ________________.

d) '. . . do you know you're a terrible child?' (line 236)

He asked me if I realised ________________.

e) 'Someone will go for her with a bread-knife one day, and he won't miss her. You must have great courage. Between ourselves, there's a lot of people I'd like to do the same to but I'd never have the nerve. Hanging is an awful death.' (lines 242-5)

He remarked that ________________. He told ________________.

He confided that ________________. He pointed out ________________.

f) 'Oh, a horrible death! Lots of the fellows I saw killed their grandmothers too, but they all said 'twas never worth it.' (lines 250-2)

He assured ________________. He went on to say ________________.

10 With the use of reported speech we would also lose the delicious immediacy of Nora bursting with incredulity and anger. As in exercise 9, change the following into indirect speech, and notice any change in effect.

a) 'Well, what did he give you?' (line 265)

She asked ________________________________.

b) 'About Gran and all?' (line 270)

She wanted to know whether ________________________.

c) 'Did you tell him you went for me with the bread-knife?' (line 274)

She asked ________________________________.

d) 'And he only gave you three Hail Marys?' (line 277)

She asked again ________________________________.

e) 'Was it the priest gave them to you?' (line 284)

She wanted to know ________________________________.

f) 'Some people have all the luck! 'Tis no advantage to anybody trying to be good. I might just as well be a sinner like you.' (lines 286-8)

She complained ________________________________.

11 Look at the paragraphs at lines 20-30 and lines 39-51. What is the effect of the introduction of sentences in direct speech into these paragraphs?

Vocabulary

Adverbial phrases with direct speech

12 The pretended feelings of Nora contrast superbly with Jackie's innocence and with the priest's well-intentioned pretence of seriousness. In the following adverbial phrases her hypocrisy is clear; where do we see her real character and where her pretended character?

		Real character	*Pretended character*
a)	in a shocked voice (line 27)	—	—
b)	in the same regretful tone (lines 92-3)	—	—
c)	with a yelp of triumph (line 108)	—	—
d)	as if butter wouldn't melt in her mouth (line 126)	—	—
e)	cocking an outraged eye (lines 184-5)	—	—
f)	with a frown (line 275)	—	—
g)	with a baffled air (line 279)	—	—

13 Which of the adverbial phrases in question 12 could be replaced by adverbs formed from adjective + *ly*?

14 Notice that if an adverb cannot be formed from an adjective, adverbial phrases can be formed as in the examples in question 12:

in a (n) + adjective + voice/tone (eg **a**, **b** from question 12)

with a (n) + noun phrase (eg **c**, **f**, **g** from question 12)

as if + clause using past tense (eg **d** from question 12)

present participle (eg **e** from question 12)

Add some words, if necessary, to the following to make adverbial phrases.

smile
excited
a look of horror
a puzzled look
he had never heard the word before
depressed
a feeling of disgust
she had just seen a ghost
laugh

15 Group work

Choose some of the following sentences. For each one, add a reporting verb and an adverbial phrase from question 14 above.

'I can't eat this!'
'What time is it?'
'Do you see what I see?'
'I know what you mean.'
'How much do you want to pay?'
'This may be the last time.'
'Good evening!'
'You must be joking!'

For example: 'What time is it?' he said *with a puzzled look.*
Give your sentences to another student, who should invent a context for the sentences. For example:

Student A: 'What time is it?' he said with a puzzled look.
Student B: This is said by a man who has taken a strong sleeping pill and just woken up. Someone has just told him the time and he can't believe it.

Extension

16 Discussion

Should children be brought up with a religion, or should they be left to choose for themselves when they are old enough?

17 Composition

The priest was very amused by the incident with Jackie. Imagine that he includes the story as an anecdote in a letter he writes to a friend. Write this part of his letter (about 150 words).

Beyond the text

Childhood and adolescence
Different narrators and points of view

18 Read the following passages (with the help of a dictionary, if necessary). As you read, identify the narrators.

a) An adult remembering his childhood — Passage __
b) A narrator who sees the world through the eyes of a child — Passage __

Passage 1: from *David Copperfield* by Charles Dickens (1850)

The first objects that assume a distinct presence before me, as I look far back into the blank of my infancy, are my mother with her pretty hair and youthful shape, and Peggotty, with no shape at all, and eyes so dark that they seemed to darken their whole neighbourhood in their face, and cheeks and arms so hard and red that I wondered the birds 5 didn't peck her in preference to apples.

I believe I can remember these two at a little distance apart, dwarfed to my sight by stooping down or kneeling on the floor, and I going unsteadily from the one to the other. I have an impression on my mind, which I cannot distinguish from actual remembrance, of the touch of 10 Peggotty's forefinger as she used to hold it out to me, and of its being roughened by needlework, like a pocket nutmeg-grater.

Passage 2: from *A Portrait of the Artist as a Young Man* by James Joyce (1915)

Once upon a time and a very good time it was there was a moocow coming down along the road and this moocow that was coming down along the road met a nicens little boy named baby tuckoo . . .

His father told him that story: his father looked at him through a glass: his father had a hairy face. 5

He was baby tuckoo. The moocow came down the road where Betty Byrne lived: she sold lemon platt.

O, the wild rose blossoms
On the little green place.

He sang that song. That was his song. 10

O, the green wothe botheth.

When you wet the bed first it is warm then it gets cold. His mother put on the oilsheet. That had the queer smell.

His mother had a nicer smell than his father. She played on the piano the sailor's hornpipe for him to dance. 15

Vocabulary

1 moocows: *baby talk for 'cow'*
3 nicens: *baby talk for 'nice'*
3 tuckoo: *an invented name for a boy*
7 lemon platt: *a kind of lemon sweet*
11 the green wothe botheth: *the child is trying to say 'the green rose blossoms'*

19 Compare the passages in more detail.

a) Is the narrator a character in the story?
b) Can you say anything about the tone of the two passages; that is, the narrator's attitude towards the events and characters described?
c) Look at passage 2. Does the narrator comment on, or interpret, what the characters say (through the use of direct speech with the addition of adverbs, or through the use of indirect speech) ? Or do the characters speak for themselves, without comment from the narrator (in direct speech)?
d) Comment on the vocabulary in the two passages. Is it simple or not? Does this give the reader a different impression of the narrator's understanding of the scene?
e) Comment on the sentences in the two passages. Are they long or short? Are they simple or complex? Does this give the reader a different impression of the narrator's understanding of the scene? If so, how does the sentence length contribute to this effect?

Author

Frank O'Connor (1903-1966) was the pseudonym adopted by Michael O'Donovan. He was born to a poor family in Cork, in the south of Ireland. He wrote literary criticism, two novels, a biography of the Irish politician Michael Collins and translations from Irish literature, but he is most famous for his short stories. These are found in the collections *Bones of Contention* (1936), *Crab Apple Jelly* (1944), *Traveller's Samples* (1951), *Domestic Relations* (1957) and *My Oedipus Complex and Other Stories* (1957), from which *First Confession* is taken. His short stories, considered among the best examples of short story writing in the twentieth century, usually reflect life among the working or middle classes in the south of Ireland. He also wrote two volumes of autobiography, *An Only Child* (1961) and *My Father's Son* (1969).

4 Romance

THE FIRST SEVEN YEARS
Bernard Malamud

Before you read

1 Which of the following statements do you agree with?

Amor vincit omnia. (Latin proverb, meaning: Love conquers everything)

'Social failure, artistic failure, sexual failure – they are all the same. And lack of money is at the bottom of them all.' (from *Keep the Aspidistra Flying* by George Orwell, 1903-1950)

It's love that makes the world go round. (popular saying)

Marry in haste, repent at leisure. (popular saying meaning: If you get married in a hurry, you will regret it)

'I don't care too much for money – money can't buy me love.' (Beatles song)

'Money don't buy everything it's true, but what it don't buy I can't use, Give me money – that's what I want.' (Beatles song)

'Oh tell her, brief is life but love is long.' (Alfred, Lord Tennyson, English poet, 1809-1892)

The First Seven Years

Feld, the shoemaker, was annoyed that his helper, Sobel, was so insensitive to his reverie that he wouldn't for a minute cease his fanatic pounding at the other bench. He gave him a look, but Sobel's bald head was bent over the last as he worked and he didn't notice. The shoemaker shrugged and continued to peer through the partly frosted 5 window at the near-sighted haze of falling February snow. Neither the shifting white blur outside, nor the sudden deep remembrance of the snowy Polish village where he had wasted his youth could turn his thoughts from Max the college boy, (a constant visitor in the mind since early that morning when Feld saw him trudging through the snowdrifts 10 on his way to school) whom he so much respected because of the sacrifices he had made throughout the years – in winter or direst heat – to further his education. An old wish returned to haunt the shoemaker: that he had had a son instead of a daughter, but this blew away in the snow for Feld, if anything, was a practical man. Yet he could not help 15 but contrast the diligence of the boy, who was a peddler's son, with Miriam's unconcern for an education. True, she was always with a book in her hand, yet when the opportunity arose for a college education, she had said no she would rather find a job. He had begged her to go, pointing out how many fathers could not afford to send their children to college, but she said she wanted to be independent. As for education, what was it, she asked, but books, which Sobel, who diligently read the classics, would as usual advise her on. Her answer greatly grieved her father. 20

A figure emerged from the snow and the door opened. At the counter the man withdrew from a wet paper bag a pair of battered shoes for repair. Who he was the shoemaker for a moment had no idea, then his heart trembled as he realized, before he had thoroughly discerned the face, that Max himself was standing there, embarrassedly explaining what he wanted done to his old shoes. Though Feld listened eagerly, he couldn't hear a word, for the opportunity that had burst upon him was deafening. 25 30

What do you think 'the opportunity' might be?

He couldn't exactly recall when the thought had occurred to him, because it was clear he had more than once considered suggesting to the boy that he go out with Miriam. But he had not dared speak, for if Max said no, how would he face him again? Or suppose Miriam, who harped so often on independence, blew up in anger and shouted at him for his meddling? Still, the chance was too good to let by: all it meant was an introduction. They might long ago have become friends had they happened to meet somewhere, therefore was it not his duty – an obligation – to bring them together, nothing more, a harmless connivance to replace an accidental encounter in the subway, let's say, or a mutual friend's introduction in the street? Just let him once see and talk to her and he would for sure be interested. As for Miriam, what possible harm for a working girl in an office, who met only loud-mouthed salesmen and illiterate shipping clerks, to make the acquaintance of a fine scholarly boy? Maybe he would awaken in her a desire to go to college; if not – the shoemaker's mind at last came to grips with the truth – let her marry an educated man and live a better life. 35 40 45

When Max finished describing what he wanted done to his shoes, Feld marked them, both with enormous holes in the soles which he pretended not to notice, with large white-chalk x's, and the rubber heels, thinned to the nails, he marked with o's, though it troubled him he might have mixed up the letters. Max inquired the price, and the shoemaker cleared his throat and asked the boy, above Sobel's insistent hammering, would he please step through the side door there into the hall. Though surprised, Max did as the shoemaker requested, and Feld went in after him. For a minute they were both silent, because Sobel had stopped banging, and it seemed they understood neither was to say anything until the noise began again. When it did, loudly, the shoemaker quickly told Max why he had asked to talk to him. 50 55 60

'Ever since you went to high school,' he said, in the dimly-lit hallway,

'I watched you in the morning go to the subway to school, and I said always to myself, this is a fine boy that he wants so much an education.'

'Thanks,' Max said, nervously alert. He was tall and grotesquely thin, with sharply cut features, particularly a beak-like nose. He was wearing a loose, long slushy overcoat that hung down to his ankles, looking like a rug draped over his bony shoulders, and a soggy, old brown hat, as battered as the shoes he had brought in. 65

'I am a business man,' the shoemaker abruptly said to conceal his embarrassment, 'so I will explain you right away why I talk to you. I have a girl, my daughter Miriam – she is nineteen – a very nice girl and also so pretty that everybody looks on her when she passes by in the street. She is smart, always with a book, and I thought to myself that a boy like you, an educated boy – I thought maybe you will be interested sometime to meet a girl like this.' He laughed a bit when he had finished and was tempted to say more but had the good sense not to. 70 75

How is Max going to react? If he is interested, what do you think he might say? And if he isn't interested, what might he say?

Max stared down like a hawk. For an uncomfortable second he was silent, then he asked, 'Did you say nineteen?'

'Yes.' 80

'Would it be all right to inquire if you have a picture of her?'

'Just a minute.' The shoemaker went into the store and hastily returned with a snapshot that Max held up to the light.

'She's all right,' he said.

Feld waited.

'And is she sensible – not the flighty kind?'

'She is very sensible.'

After another short pause, Max said it was okay with him if he met her.

'Here is my telephone,' said the shoemaker, hurriedly handing him a slip of paper. 'Call her up. She comes home from work six o'clock.'

Max folded the paper and tucked it away into his worn leather wallet.

'About the shoes,' he said. 'How much did you say they will cost me?'

'Don't worry about the price.'

'I just like to have an idea.'

'A dollar – dollar fifty. A dollar fifty,' the shoemaker said.

At once he felt bad, for he usually charged two twenty-five for this kind of job. Either he should have asked the regular price or done the work for nothing.

Later, as he entered the store, he was startled by a violent clanging and looked up to see Sobel pounding with all his might upon the naked last. It broke, the iron striking the floor and jumping with a thump against the wall, but before the enraged shoemaker could cry out, the assistant had torn his hat and coat from the hook and rushed out into the snow.

> *Can you explain Sobel's behaviour? How many motives can you think of?*

So Feld, who had looked forward to anticipating how it would go with his daughter and Max, instead had a great worry on his mind. Without his temperamental helper he was a lost man, especially since it was years now that he had carried the store alone. The shoemaker had for an age suffered from a heart condition that threatened collapse if he dared exert himself. Five years ago, after an attack, it had appeared as though he would have either to sacrifice his business upon the auction block and live on a pittance thereafter, or put himself at the mercy of some unscrupulous employee who would in the end probably ruin him. But just at the moment of his darkest despair, this Polish refugee, Sobel, appeared one night from the street and begged for work. He was a stocky man, poorly dressed, with a bald head that had once been blond, a severely plain face and soft blue eyes prone to tears over the sad books he read, a young man but old – no one would have guessed thirty. Though he confessed he knew nothing of shoemaking, he said he was apt and would work for a very little if Feld taught him the trade. Thinking that with, after all, a landsman, he would have less to fear than from a complete stranger, Feld took him on and within six weeks the refugee rebuilt as good a shoe as he, and not long thereafter expertly ran the business for the thoroughly relieved shoemaker.

Feld could trust him with anything and did, frequently going home after an hour or two at the store, leaving all the money in the till, knowing Sobel would guard every cent of it. The amazing thing was that he demanded so little. His wants were few; in money he wasn't interested – in nothing but books, it seemed – which he one by one lent to Miriam, together with his profuse, queer written comments, manufactured during his lonely rooming house evenings, thick pads of commentary which the shoemaker peered at and twitched his shoulders over as his daughter, from her fourteenth year, read page by sanctified page, as if the word of God were inscribed on them. To protect Sobel, Feld himself had to see that he received more than he asked for. Yet his conscience bothered him for not insisting that the assistant accept a better wage than he was getting, though Feld had honestly told him he could earn a handsome salary if he worked elsewhere, or maybe opened a place of his own. But the assistant answered, somewhat ungraciously, that he was not interested in going elsewhere, and though Feld frequently asked himself what keeps him here? why does he stay? he finally answered it that the man, no doubt because of his terrible experiences as a refugee, was afraid of the world.

> *Can you answer Feld's questions? What* does *keep Sobel there?*

After the incident with the broken last, angered by Sobel's behaviour, the shoemaker decided to let him stew for a week in the rooming house, although his own strength was taxed dangerously and the business suffered. However, after several sharp nagging warnings from both his wife and daughter, he went finally in search of Sobel, as he had once before, quite recently, when over some fancied slight – Feld had merely asked him not to give Miriam so many books to read because her eyes were strained and red – the assistant had left the place in a huff, an incident which, as usual, came to nothing for he had returned after the shoemaker had talked to him, and taken his seat at the bench. But this time, after Feld had plodded through the snow to Sobel's house – he had thought of sending Miriam but the idea became repugnant to him – the burly landlady at the door informed him in a nasal voice that Sobel was not at home, and though Feld knew this was a nasty lie, for where had the refugee to go? still for some reason he was not completely sure of – it may have been the cold and his fatigue – he decided not to insist on seeing him. Instead he went home and hired a new helper.

Having settled the matter, though not entirely to his satisfaction, for he had much more to do than before, and so, for example, could no longer lie late in bed mornings because he had to get up to open the store for the new assistant, a speechless, dark man with an irritating rasp as he worked, whom he would not trust with the key as he had Sobel. Furthermore, this one, though able to do a fair repair job, knew nothing of grades of leather or prices, so Feld had to make his own purchases; and every night at closing time it was necessary to count the money in the till and lock up. However, he was not dissatisfied, for he lived much in his thoughts of Max and Miriam. The college boy had called her, and they had arranged a meeting for this coming Friday night. The shoemaker would personally have preferred Saturday, which he felt would make it a date of the first magnitude, but he learned Friday was Miriam's choice, so he said nothing. The day of the week did not matter. What mattered was the aftermath. Would they like each other and want to be friends? He sighed at all the time that would have to go by before he knew for sure. Often he was tempted to talk to Miriam about the boy, to ask whether she thought she would like his type – he had told her only that he considered Max a nice boy and had suggested he call her – but the one time he tried she snapped at him – justly – how should she know? 175 180

At last Friday came. Feld was not feeling particularly well so he stayed in bed, and Mrs. Feld thought it better to remain in the bedroom with him when Max called. Miriam received the boy, and her parents could hear their voices, his throaty one, as they talked. Just before leaving, Miriam brought Max to the bedroom door and he stood there a minute, a tall, slightly hunched figure wearing a thick, droopy suit, and apparently at ease as he greeted the shoemaker and his wife, which was surely a good sign. And Miriam, although she had worked all day, looked fresh and pretty. She was a large-framed girl with a well-shaped body, and she had a fine open face and soft hair. They made, Feld thought, a first-class couple. 185 190

Will the evening be a success or not, do you think? Point to evidence in the story so far to support your opinion.

Miriam returned after 11:30. Her mother was already asleep, but the shoemaker got out of bed and after locating his bathrobe went into the kitchen, where Miriam, to his surprise, sat at the table, reading. 195

'So where did you go?' Feld asked pleasantly.

'For a walk,' she said, not looking up.

'I advised him,' Feld said, clearing his throat, 'he shouldn't spend so much money.' 200

'I didn't care.'

The shoemaker boiled up some water for tea and sat down at the table with a cupful and a thick slice of lemon.

'So how,' he sighed after a sip, 'did you enjoy?'

'It was all right.' 205

He was silent. She must have sensed his disappointment, for she added, 'You can't really tell much the first time.'

'You will see him again?'

Turning a page, she said that Max had asked for another date.

'For when?' 210

'Saturday.'

'So what did you say?'

'What did I say?' she asked, delaying for a moment – 'I said yes.'

Afterwards she inquired about Sobel, and Feld, without exactly knowing why, said the assistant had got another job. Miriam said nothing more and began to read. The shoemaker's conscience did not trouble him; he was satisfied with the Saturday date. 215

> *How do you think Miriam's relationship with Max might develop?*

During the week, by placing here and there a deft question, he managed to get from Miriam some information about Max. It surprised him to learn that the boy was not studying to be either a doctor or lawyer but was taking a business course leading to a degree in accountancy. Feld was a little disappointed because he thought of accountants as bookkeepers and would have preferred 'a higher profession'. However, it was not long before he had investigated the subject and discovered that Certified Public Accountants were highly respected people, so he was thoroughly content as Saturday approached. But because Saturday was a busy day, he was much in the store and therefore did not see Max when he came to call for Miriam. From his wife he learned there had been nothing especially revealing about their meeting. Max had rung the bell and Miriam had got her coat and left with him – nothing more. Feld did not probe, for his wife was not particularly observant. Instead, he waited up for Miriam with a newspaper on his lap, which he scarcely looked at so lost was he in thinking of the future. He awoke to find her in the room with him, tiredly removing her hat. Greeting her, he was suddenly inexplicably afraid to ask anything about the evening. But since she volunteered nothing he was at last forced to inquire how she had enjoyed herself. Miriam began something non-committal but apparently changed her mind, for she said after a minute, 'I was bored.'

When Feld had sufficiently recovered from his anguished disappointment to ask why, she answered without hesitation, 'Because he's nothing more than a materialist.'

'What means this word?'

'He has no soul. He's only interested in things.'

He considered her statement for a long time but then asked, 'Will you see him again?'

'He didn't ask.'

'Suppose he will ask you?'

'I won't see him.'

He did not argue; however, as the days went by he hoped increasingly she would change her mind. He wished the boy would telephone, because he was sure there was more to him than Miriam, with her inexperienced eye, could discern. But Max didn't call. As a matter of fact he took a different route to school, no longer passing the shoemaker's store, and Feld was deeply hurt.

Then one afternoon Max came in and asked for his shoes. The shoemaker took them down from the shelf where he had placed them, apart from the other pairs. He had done the work himself and the soles and heels were well built and firm. The shoes had been highly polished and somehow looked better than new. Max's Adam's apple went up once when he saw them, and his eyes had little lights in them.

'How much?' he asked, without directly looking at the shoemaker.

'Like I told you before,' Feld answered sadly. 'One dollar fifty cents.'

Max handed him two crumpled bills and received in return a newly-minted silver half dollar.

He left. Miriam had not been mentioned. That night the shoemaker discovered that his new assistant had been all the while stealing from him, and he suffered a heart attack. 265

Though the attack was very mild, he lay in bed for three weeks. Miriam spoke of going for Sobel, but sick as he was Feld rose in wrath against the idea. Yet in his heart he knew there was no other way, and the first weary day back in the shop thoroughly convinced him, so that night after supper he dragged himself to Sobel's rooming house. 270

He toiled up the stairs, though he knew it was bad for him, and at the top knocked at the door. Sobel opened it and the shoemaker entered. The room was a small, poor one, with a single window facing the street. It contained a narrow cot, a low table and several stacks of books piled haphazardly around on the floor along the wall, which made him think how queer Sobel was, to be uneducated and read so much. He had once asked him, Sobel, why you read so much? and the assistant could not answer him. Did you ever study in a college someplace? he had asked, but Sobel shook his head. He read, he said, to know. But to know what, the shoemaker demanded, and to know, why? Sobel never explained, which proved he read much because he was queer. 275 280

Feld sat down to recover his breath. The assistant was resting on his bed with his heavy back to the wall. His shirt and trousers were clean, and his stubby fingers, away from the shoemaker's bench, were strangely pallid. His face was thin and pale, as if he had been shut in this room since the day he had bolted from the store. 285

> *What do you think this conversation will be like – what will they say to each other?*

'So when you will come back to work?' Feld asked him.

To his surprise, Sobel burst out, 'Never.' 290

Jumping up, he strode over to the window that looked out upon the miserable street. 'Why should I come back?' he cried.

'I will raise your wages.'

'Who cares for your wages!'

The shoemaker, knowing he didn't care, was at a loss what else to say. 295

'What do you want from me, Sobel?'

'Nothing.'

'I always treated you like you was my son.'

Sobel vehemently denied it. 'So why you look for strange boys in the street they should go out with Miriam? Why you don't think of me?' 300

The shoemaker's hands and feet turned freezing cold. His voice became so hoarse he couldn't speak. At last he cleared his throat and croaked, 'So what has my daughter got to do with a shoemaker thirty-five years old who works for me?' 305

'Why do you think I worked so long for you?' Sobel cried out. 'For the stingy wages I sacrificed five years of my life so you could have to eat and drink and where to sleep?'

'Then for what?' shouted the shoemaker.

'For Miriam,' he blurted – 'for her.' 310

The shoemaker, after a time, managed to say, 'I pay wages in cash, Sobel,' and lapsed into silence. Though he was seething with excitement, his mind was coldly clear, and he had to admit to himself he had sensed all along that Sobel felt this way. He had never so much as thought it consciously, but he had felt it and was afraid. 315

'Miriam knows?' he muttered hoarsely.

'She knows.'

'You told her?'

'No.'

Then how does she know?' 320

'How does she know?' Sobel said, 'because she knows. She knows who I am and what is in my heart.'

Feld had a sudden insight. In some devious way, with his books and commentary, Sobel had given Miriam to understand that he loved her. The shoemaker felt a terrible anger at him for his deceit. 325

'Sobel, you are crazy,' he said bitterly. 'She will never marry a man so old and ugly like you.'

Sobel turned black with rage. He cursed the shoemaker, but then, though he trembled to hold it in, his eyes filled with tears and he broke into deep sobs. With his back to Feld, he stood at the window, fists 330 clenched, and his shoulders shook with his choked sobbing.

Things between Feld and Sobel have obviously reached a crisis.
What will they say to each other now, do you think?

Watching him, the shoemaker's anger diminished. His teeth were on edge with pity for the man, and his eyes grew moist. How strange and sad that a refugee, a grown man, bald and old with his miseries, who had by the skin of his teeth escaped Hitler's incinerators, should fall in 335 love, when he had got to America, with a girl less than half his age. Day after day, for five years he had sat at his bench, cutting and hammering away, waiting for the girl to become a woman, unable to ease his heart with speech, knowing no protest but desperation.

'Ugly I didn't mean,' he said half aloud. 340

Then he realized that what he had called ugly was not Sobel but Miriam's life if she married him. He felt for his daughter a strange and gripping sorrow, as if she were already Sobel's bride, the wife, after all, of a shoemaker, and had in her life no more than her mother had had. And all his dreams for her – why he had slaved and destroyed his heart 345 with anxiety and labor – all these dreams of a better life were dead.

The room was quiet. Sobel was standing by the window reading, and it was curious that when he read he looked young.

'She is only nineteen,' Feld said brokenly. 'This is too young yet to get married. Don't ask her for two years more, till she is twenty-one, then you can talk to her.' 350

Sobel didn't answer. Feld rose and left. He went slowly down the stairs but once outside, though it was an icy night and the crisp falling snow whitened the street, he walked with a stronger stride.

But the next morning, when the shoemaker arrived, heavy-hearted, to open the store, he saw he needn't have come, for his assistant was already seated at the last, pounding leather for his love. 355

See Glossary section at the back of the book for vocabulary.

First reaction

2 a) What do you feel at the end of this story – a sense of triumph for Sobel, sadness for Feld, or a mixture of both?

b) Do you feel apprehensive about Miriam's future, or optimistic for her and Sobel?

Close reading

Examining characterisation

3 Max

a) Look at the first meeting between Max and Feld (lines 62-96). What are the details that make the reader suspicious of Max?

b) Look at the second meeting (lines 255-64). What physical details give the reader an impression of what Max is thinking and how he is feeling? Describe in your own words what is going through his head during this meeting.

4 Sobel

a) Sobel is often shown working. Find examples of this in the story. Why does he work so hard? Think of as many reasons as you can.

b) Does Malamud make Sobel a sympathetic character? Support your choice with references to the story.

5 Feld

a) Feld is often shown as a 'materialist' – he thinks a lot about money. Find examples of this in the story.

b) Consequently, how do we judge Feld – do we dismiss him as a materialist (as Miriam dismisses Max), or do we judge him more kindly?

c) 'Max handed him two crumpled bills and received in return a newly-minted silver half dollar.' (lines 263-4)
Is there any significance in the way the money is described here?

d) **i)** There are two phrases expressing Feld's feelings at the end of the story (lines 352-end) that seem contradictory – what are they?
ii) Can you explain why he feels like this?

Language practice

Speculating about future developments – (Conditional sentences type 2)
if + past tense, . . . *would/might* + base form of verb

One of the ways that Malamud shows us Feld's character and his anxiety is by allowing us to hear him think, to observe him as he constantly and obsessively imagines all kinds of future developments.

6 Look at lines 33-49. Quote the sentences from the story that match the following statements.

a) Max would certainly want to see Miriam again if he was given the chance to meet and talk to her.
b) If Feld suggested to Miriam that she went out with Max she might react angrily and accuse him of interfering.
c) Miriam would have a better life if she married Max than if she married someone from her office.
d) If Feld suggested that Max went out with Miriam he might not like the idea. And if Max didn't take up his suggestion Feld would find it very difficult to speak to him again.
e) If Miriam met Max she might become interested in continuing her education.

What is the difference between *would* and *might*?

7 Look at lines 106-44, where we see Feld worried about his business. Imagine that the following paragraph represents the thoughts running through Feld's mind. Choose the best form of the verb in brackets: past tense, or *would/might* + base form of verb.

If I (**1** ask) __________ Sobel to come back to the shop immediately, business (**2** not suffer) __________ and I (**3** not feel) __________ so bad – but if I (**4** do) __________ that he (**5** not realise) __________ that this time I'm really angry. Of course if I

(**6** dismiss) __________ Sobel he (**7** be) __________ all right: he (**8** definitely earn) __________ more money somewhere else, or he (**9** even open) __________ his own business. But what about me? I (**10** have to) __________ hire somebody else if he (**11** not be) __________ here. I (**12** be) __________ lucky with a new assistant, but on the other hand if I (**13** have) __________ the bad luck to get a dishonest one he (**14** steal) __________ from me. Then there's the possibility of selling the business. I (**15** get) __________ some money if I (**16** auction) __________ the shop but I (**17** not be able) __________ to earn any more, and I (**18** have to) __________ live off the money I got from the sale for the rest of my life. My income (**19** be) __________ even smaller than it is now if I (**20** do) __________ that. What shall I do?

8 Here are some ideas to help you speculate on the future of the three main characters. Form questions from the prompts, and then discuss your answers.

a) If Feld/ordered Miriam not to talk to Sobel how/she react? How/Sobel react?
b) If Feld/have second thoughts and dismiss Sobel what/Sobel do? What Miriam do?
c) How/Feld feel if Sobel and Miriam ran away together?
d) What/Sobel do if Miriam reject him?
e) If Sobel and Miriam get married/they be happy? What kind/ life/they have?/They still be happy if/they never have enough money?
f) Miriam have a 'better' life/if she marry a man with career prospects?

Example
If Feld ordered Miriam not to talk to Sobel how would she react?
I think she would . . . . . .
Really? I think she might . . . . . .

Vocabulary

Describing people

In this story, as in many stories, we form an opinion of the characters not only by judging their behaviour and what they say, but also by reacting to physical descriptions.

Look at Malamud's descriptions of Sobel and Max.

Sobel

bald head (line 3)
a stocky man, poorly dressed, with a bald head that had once been blond, a severely plain face and soft blue eyes prone to tears over the sad books he read, a young man but old (lines 116-19)

his heavy back to the wall. His shirt and trousers were clean, and his stubby fingers . . . were strangely pallid. His face was thin and pale (lines 285-7)

old and ugly [Feld says] (line 327)

bald and old with his miseries [Feld thinks] (line 334)

when he read he looked young [Feld thinks] (line 348)

Max

He was tall and grotesquely thin, with sharply cut features, particularly a beak-like nose. He was wearing a loose, long slushy overcoat that hung down to his ankles, looking like a rug draped over his bony shoulders, and a soggy, old brown hat, as battered as the shoes he had brought in. (lines 65-9)

Max stared down like a hawk. (line 78)

his throaty one [voice] (line 186)

a tall, slightly hunched figure wearing a thick, droopy suit (line 188)

9 The description of each man is contradictory. For example, Sobel is 'a young man but old'. The dominant impression that the reader gets of each man is one of conflicting qualities. What other contradictions can you find?

10 With the physical descriptions above Malamud doesn't *tell* us anything explicit about the characters of Max and Sobel, but he *shows* us something from which we form an impression of their characters. Keeping in mind these physical descriptions, which of the following words, in your opinion, give an impression of the character of each man? Sort the words into lists and explain the reasons for your choice.

sad sinister pathetic vulnerable reliable stupid
cruel humorous awkward spiritual untrustworthy
honest unpleasant mean insecure sensitive
insensitive clever

	Description	*Reason*
Max	______________________	______________________
	______________________	______________________
	______________________	______________________
	______________________	______________________
Sobel	______________________	______________________
	______________________	______________________
	______________________	______________________
	______________________	______________________
Neither	______________________	______________________
	______________________	______________________
	______________________	______________________
	______________________	______________________

11 a) The most frequent adjectives that Malamud uses to describe Max and Sobel are very common ones (tall, bold, old, thin), so how does he manage to suggest value judgements on their characters? He does it in several ways:

i) by qualifying the adjectives with adverbs or other adjectives that give a value judgement:
Max is *grotesquely* thin (and therefore unpleasant).
Sobel is *severely* plain (and therefore honest).
Sobel has *soft* blue eyes *prone to tears* (and therefore knows what emotion is).

ii) by comparison with something (or somebody) else:
a *beak-like* nose . . . Max stared down *like a hawk* (and is therefore predatory)
or by comparison with another state:
when he read he *looked young* (and therefore his normal external appearance does not always show his real self)

iii) by giving background information that modifies and explains the present: a bald head *that had once been blond,* . . . bald and old *with his miseries*

b) Consider also how Malamud describes their clothes. Look at lines 66-9, 188, 285. Does this add to their character description? How?

12 Describe the people in the pictures opposite in two ways.

a) So that you give a positive impression of their characters.
b) So that you give a negative impression of their characters.

Try to *show* the reader what the person is like through your physical description rather than *tell* the reader about the person's character.

Extension

13 Discussion

Which of the following statements do you agree with? Although they are based on the story, you can extend the discussion to include other examples from literature and from life.

Miriam and Sobel should get married straight away. Love should not have to wait.

As Feld reluctantly suggests, Miriam and Sobel should wait for a couple of years before thinking of getting married. If they really love each other, a couple of years will make no difference.

14 Composition

Imagine that Feld decides to dismiss Sobel and forbids him to see Miriam. Write the letter that Sobel would send to Miriam.

Beyond the text

A lover's description

15 Look at this poem by the English poet Barry Cole (born 1936). The situation seems to be that a man goes to a police station to report that his lover is missing, and the policeman asks him for a description of her. From the twenty-one words in the box below choose the ten words that have been cut out of the poem.

anyone teeth nose description black
distinctive texture person breath lips blue
terrible eyes habits kisses ankles mouth
smell hair black no-one

Reported missing

Can you give me a precise description?
Said the policeman. Her (**1**) __________, I told him,
Were soft. Could you give me, he said, pencil
Raised, a metaphor? Soft as an open mouth,
I said. Were there any noticeable 5
Peculiarities? he asked. Her (**2**) __________ hung
Heavily, I said. Any particular
Colour? he said. I told him I could recall
Little but its (**3**) __________ scent. What do
You mean, he asked, by distinctive? It had 10

The (**4**) __________ of woman's hair, I said. Where
Were you? he asked. Closer than I am to
(**5**) __________ at present, I said, level
With her mouth, level with her eyes. Her (**6**) __________?
He said, what about her eyes? There were two, 15
I said, both (**7**) __________. It has been established,
He said, that eyes cannot, outside common
usage, be black; are you implying that
Violence was used? Only the gentle
Hammer blow of her (**8**) __________, the scent 20
Of her (**9**) __________, the . . . Quite, said the policeman,
Standing, but I regret that we know of
No one answering to that (**10**) __________

Line 18: 'a black eye' in English means that there is a bruise around the eye.

16 This poem plays with the expectations of the reader.

a) Should we read the poem as a real narrative, do you think? Is the poet's lover really missing?

b) Or is the poem a metaphor? Has the poet's lover left him, and he uses the idea of reporting her missing at the police station as a metaphor describing his desperation at losing her?

17 a) What language does the policeman use that seems the particular language of policemen?

b) Does he say anything that it would be unlikely for a policeman to say?

c) Why do you think the poem ends as it does?

Author

Bernard Malamud (1914-1986) was born in Brooklyn, New York, and was educated at City College, New York, and Columbia University. Malamud was a writer of short stories and novels. His fourth novel, *The Fixer* (1966), won a Pulitzer Prize (one of the most important American awards for literature and journalism). It is about a Jewish handyman (a 'fixer') in Russia before the First World War who, falsely accused of murder, becomes a victim of anti-Semitism. It was filmed by John Frankenheimer, starring Alan Bates. *The Natural*, his first novel (see Chapter 7, Beyond the text) was filmed starring Robert Redford. His volumes of short stories include *Idiots First* and *The Magic Barrel* (1958), from which *The First Seven Years* is taken.

5 Fairy Tales

THE NIGHTINGALE AND THE ROSE
Oscar Wilde

Before you read

1 The fairy tale belongs to folk literature and is part of the oral tradition. And yet no one bothered to record them until the brothers Grimm produced their famous collection of *Haus-Märchen* or *Household Tales* (1812, 1815, 1822).

In its written form the fairy tale tends to be a narrative in prose about the fortunes and misfortunes of a hero or heroine who, having experienced various adventures of a more or less supernatural kind, lives happily ever after. Magic, charms, disguise and spells are some of the major ingredients of such stories, which are often subtle in their interpretation of human nature and psychology.

(from J A Cuddon), *A Dictionary of Literary Terms*, (Penguin, 1982)

Is there anything you want to add to, or take away from, this definition? What fairy stories do you know? Some common European ones are *Puss in Boots, Cinderella, Red Riding Hood.*

The Nightingale and the Rose

'She said that she would dance with me if I brought her red roses', cried the young Student, 'but in all my garden there is no red rose'.

From her nest in the holm-oak tree the Nightingale heard him and she looked out through the leaves and wondered.

'No red rose in all my garden!' he cried, and his beautiful eyes filled with tears. 'Ah, on what little things does happiness depend! I have read all that the wise men have written, and all the secrets of philosophy are mine, yet for want of a red rose is my life made wretched.' 5

'Here at last is a true lover', said the Nightingale. 'Night after night have I sung of him, though I knew him not: night after night have I told his story to the stars and now I see him. His hair is dark as the Hyacinth-blossom, and his lips are red as the rose of his desire; but passion has made his face like pale ivory, and sorrow has set her seal upon his brow'. 10

'The Prince gives a ball to-morrow night', murmured the young Student, 'and my love will be of the company. If I bring her a red rose she will dance with me till dawn. If I bring her a red rose, I shall hold her in my arms, and she will lean her head upon my shoulder, and her hand will be clasped in mine. But there is no red rose in my garden, so I shall 15

her nest in his branches. 'Sing me one last song', he whispered; 'I shall feel lonely when you are gone'.

So the Nightingale sang to the Oak-tree, and her voice was like water bubbling from a silver jar. 110

When she had finished her song, the Student got up, and pulled a note-book and a lead-pencil out of his pocket.

How do you think the student will react to the nightingale's song?

'She has form', he said to himself, as he walked away through the grove, 'that cannot be denied to her; but has she got feeling? I am afraid not. In fact, she is like most artists; she is all style without any sincerity. She would not sacrifice herself for others. She thinks merely of music, and everybody knows that the arts are selfish. Still, it must be admitted that she has some beautiful notes in her voice. What a pity it is that they do not mean anything, or do any practical good!' and he went to his room, and lay down on his little pallet-bed, and began to think of his love; and, after a time, he fell asleep. 115 120

And when the moon shone in the heavens the Nightingale flew to the Rose-tree, and set her breast against the thorn. All night long she sang, with her breast against the thorn, and the cold crystal Moon leaned down and listened. All night long she sang, and the thorn went deeper into her breast, and her life-blood ebbed away from her. 125

She sang first of the birth of love in the heart of a boy and a girl. And on the topmost spray of the Rose-tree there blossomed a marvellous rose, petal following petal, as song followed song. Pale was it, at first, as the mist that hangs over the river, pale as the feet of morning, and silver as the wings of the dawn. As the shadow of a rose in a mirror of silver, as the shadow of a rose in a waterpool, so was the rose that blossomed on the topmost spray of the Tree. 130

But the Tree cried to the Nightingale to press closer against the thorn. 'Press closer, little Nightingale', cried the Tree, 'or the Day will come before the rose is finished'. 135

So the Nightingale pressed closer against the thorn, and louder and louder grew her song, for she sang of the birth of passion in the soul of a man and a maid. 140

And a delicate flush of pink came into the leaves of the rose, like the flush in the face of the bridegroom when he kisses the lips of the bride. But the thorn had not yet reached her heart so the rose's heart remained white, for only a Nightingale's heart's-blood can crimson the heart of a rose. 145

And the Tree cried to the Nightingale to press closer against the thorn. 'Press closer, little Nightingale', cried the Tree, 'or the Day will come before the rose is finished'.

So the Nightingale pressed closer against the thorn, and the thorn touched her heart, and a fierce pang of pain shot through her. Bitter, bitter was the pain, and wilder and wilder grew her song, for she sang of the Love that is perfected by Death, of the Love that dies not in the tomb. 150

And the marvellous rose became crimson, like the rose of the eastern sky. Crimson was the girdle of petals, and crimson as a ruby was the heart. 155

But the Nightingale's voice grew fainter, and her little wings began to beat, and a film came over her eyes. Fainter and fainter grew her song, and she felt something choking her in her throat.

Then she gave one last burst of music. The white Moon heard it, and she forgot the dawn, and lingered on in the sky. The red rose heard it, 160 and trembled all over with ecstasy, and opened its petals in the cold morning air. Echo brought it to her purple cavern in the hills, and woke the sleeping shepherds from their dreams. It floated through the reeds of the river, and they carried its message to the sea.

'Look, look!' cried the Tree, 'the rose is finished now'; but the 165 Nightingale made no answer, for she was lying dead in the long grass, with the thorn in her heart.

And at noon the Student opened his window and looked out.

How do you think the student will react when he sees the red rose?

'Why, what a wonderful piece of luck!' he cried; 'here is a red rose. I have never seen any rose like it in all my life. It is so beautiful that I am 170 sure it has a long Latin name'; and he leaned down and plucked it.

Then he put on his hat, and ran up to the Professor's house with the rose in his hand.

The daughter of the Professor was sitting in the doorway winding blue silk on a reel, and her little dog was lying at her feet. 175

'You said that you would dance with me if I brought you a red rose', cried the Student. 'Here is the reddest rose in all the world. You will wear it to-night next your heart, and as we dance together it will tell you how I love you'.

What do you think the girl's reaction will be?

But the girl frowned. 180

'I am afraid it will not go with my dress', she answered; 'and besides, the Chamberlain's nephew has sent me some real jewels, and everybody knows that jewels cost far more than flowers'.

'Well, upon my word, you are very ungrateful', said the Student angrily; and he threw the rose into the street, where it fell into the 185 gutter, and a cartwheel went over it.

'Ungrateful!' said the girl. 'I tell you what, you are very rude; and after all, who are you? Only a Student. Why, I don't believe you have even got silver buckles to your shoes as the Chamberlain's nephew has'; and she got up from her chair and went into the house. 190

'What a silly thing Love is!' said the Student as he walked away. 'It is not half as useful as logic, for it does not prove anything, and it is always telling one of things that are not going to happen, and making one believe things that are not true. In fact, it is quite unpractical, and, as in this age to be practical is everything, I shall go back to Philosophy and study Metaphysics'. 195

So he returned to his room and pulled out a great dusty book, and began to read.

First reaction

2 Fairy tales often end with a moral that gives an interpretation of the story. Choose one of the following morals for *The Nightingale and the Rose*, or make up a moral of your own.

a) Love should be avoided: it is useless and impractical.
b) Never get emotionally involved in other people's affairs.
c) Love is almost always skin-deep.
d) People don't notice the most generous acts.
e) Be cynical about life if you don't want to get hurt.
f) Be romantic and idealistic, even if other people don't notice or care.

Your moral ________________________________

Close reading

Sequencing the events of a story

3 Here is a summary of *The Nightingale and the Rose*, but the descriptions of what happens – in the right hand column – are not in order. Match the descriptions in the right hand column with the lines in the left hand column.

lines:

1) 1-34
2) 35-45
3) 46-74
4) 75-84
5) 85-91
6) 92-103
7) 104-11
8) 112-22
9) 123-67
10) 168-79
11) 180-90
12) 191-8

a) The nightingale tells the student her decision.
b) Various characters in the student's garden give their opinions of the student's unhappiness.
c) The student finds the rose and takes it to the girl.
d) The nightingale hears how she can get a red rose.
e) The student comments on the nightingale's singing.
f) The nightingale sings a last song to the oak tree.
g) The student gives a final comment on love.
h) The student describes his unhappiness, and the nightingale listens.
i) The nightingale makes the rose.
j) The girl rejects the student's rose.
k) The nightingale decides to sacrifice herself.

l) The nightingale tries unsuccessfully to find a red rose.

1) — 2) — 3) — 4) — 5) — 6) — 7) — 8) — 9) — 10) — 11) — 12) —

4 In fairy stories the number *three* is very important. There are very often three brothers or sisters, or three animals, or things tend to happen three times. In *The Nightingale and the Rose* there are three minor characters – the Lizard, the Butterfly and the Daisy – with their three questions (lines 35-40). Can you find another example of something happening three times in the story? Can you think of examples from other stories you know?

5 The style becomes much plainer, much less poetic, after line 167. Can you suggest a reason why?

Language practice

Using linking devices in narrative – Conjunctions, relative pronouns and adverbs

6 Retell the story by completing the following paragraph. Use the words in the box to fill in the gaps. Try not to refer back to the story.

so as then which after this time because reluctantly eventually however while despite but who by now and because of the next day unfortunately soon

There was once a young student (**1**) ______ was in love with the daughter of a Professor, (**2**) ______ she had said that she would only dance with him at the Prince's ball if he brought her red roses. (**3**) ______, the student had no red roses in his garden. (**4**) ______ he was crying in his garden a nightingale heard him and felt sorry for him (**5**) ______ she believed that he was a true lover. She decided to help him, and flew to a rose tree to get him the rose he needed. But this rose tree had only white roses. (**6**) ______ she went to another rose tree, but this one had only yellow roses (**7**) ______ suggested she tried another tree. (**8**) ______ she found a rose tree (**9**) ______ grew red roses but this year, (**10**) ______ the severe winter, it didn't have any roses. (**11**) ______ the nightingale was beginning to despair, and begged the rose tree to tell her how to get a red rose. (**12**) ______, the rose tree explained that she would have to kill herself by pressing against a thorn while singing. (**13**) ______ a moment's thought the nightingale decided to do this, and went to the student to tell him that everything was going to be all right. (**14**) ______ the passion in the nightingale's song, the student couldn't understand her message; he thought it was just a pretty but meaningless piece of music. (**15**) ______ night came, and the nightingale flew to the rose tree and sang all night pressing against a thorn, (**16**) ______ she had promised, until she died. (**17**) ______ the student found that a single red rose had grown miraculously during the night. Overjoyed, he rushed to the Professor's house to give the rose to the girl and remind her of her promise. The girl, (**18**) ______, was more impressed by the jewels sent to her by the Chamberlain's nephew than by the poor student's flower, (**19**) ______ they quarrelled. Disillusioned, the student went home, where he (**20**) ______ forgot about the girl and returned once more to his books.

Do you agree with this summary of the story, or is there anything you would like to add or take away?

Vocabulary

Describing personal qualities
Abstract nouns and adjectives

7 You might recognise the following qualities in the characters in Wilde's story. What are the adjectives that describe these qualities? Use a dictionary if necessary.

Quality	Adjective	Quality	Adjective
ingratitude	______	vanity	______
idealism	______	sympathy	______
unselfishness	______	romanticism	______
superficiality	______	generosity	______
materialism	______	lack of imagination	______

8 Which of the adjectives you have just formed could apply to the main characters, or to their behaviour at moments in the story?

Fill in the following table, in each case referring to a sentence or episode from the story to support your decision. You can use the same adjective for two characters, if you think it is suitable.

The student	The nightingale	The girl

Which *one* adjective would you choose to describe each character?

9 Here are some more adjectives of character. This time decide how the noun is formed from the adjective and write the noun in the appropriate column in the table.

compassionate practical tender cynical
sensitive sentimental kind realistic shallow
educated rude passionate sincere insincere
egocentric unhappy

-ity	-ion	-ness	-ism
practicality			

10 Consider all the personal qualities you have discussed in this section. Which of these qualities do you look for in people? Which do you find the most attractive and which the most unpleasant? Choose the **three** best and **three** worst qualities in your opinion. Here are some ways of talking about your decisions.

I think people should be sincere.
I like people to be sincere.
I think sincerity is important in a person.

I can't stand insincere people.
I hate people who are insincere.
I can't bear insincerity.

Do you recognise any of these qualities in yourself?

OUTSIDE THE CABINET-MAKER'S
F Scott Fitzgerald

Before you read

11 Once upon a time there was a King and Queen who had a beautiful daughter. But an Ogre captured them all and kept them as prisoners. . . .
(an ogre is a monstrous giant in fairy stories)

Finish this very short fairy story in two or three sentences. You must use the words *Prince, three magic stones, rescue.*

Outside the Cabinet-Maker's

The automobile stopped at the corner of Sixteenth and some dingy-looking street. The lady got out. The man and the little girl stayed in the car.

'I'm going to tell him it can't cost more than twenty dollars,' said the lady. 5

'All right. Have you the plans?'

'Oh, yes' – she reached for her bag in the back seat – 'at least I have now.'

'Dites qu'il ne faut pas avoir les forts placards,' said the man.

'Ni le bon bois.' 10

'All right.'

'I wish you wouldn't talk French,' said the little girl.

'Et il faut avoir un bon 'height.' L'un des Murphys était comme ça.'

He held his hand five feet from the ground. The lady went through a door lettered 'Cabinet-Maker' and disappeared up a small stairs. 15

> *What do you think they are talking about? What is this thing that shouldn't cost more than twenty dollars?*

The man and the little girl looked around unexpectantly. The neighborhood was red brick, vague, quiet. There were a few darkies doing something or other up the street and an occasional automobile went by. It was a fine November day.

'Listen,' said the man to the little girl, 'I love you.' 20

'I love you too,' said the little girl, smiling politely.

'Listen,' the man continued. 'Do you see that house over the way?'

The little girl looked. It was a flat in back of a shop. Curtains masked most of its interior, but there was a faint stir behind them. On one

window a loose shutter banged from back to forth every few minutes. Neither the man nor the little girl had ever seen the place before.

'There's a Fairy Princess behind those curtains,' said the man. 'You can't see her but she's there, kept concealed by an Ogre. Do you know what an Ogre is?'

'Yes.'

'Well, this Princess is very beautiful with long golden hair.'

They both regarded the house. Part of a yellow dress appeared momentarily in the window.

'That's her,' the man said. 'The people who live there are guarding her for the Ogre. He's keeping the King and Queen prisoner ten thousand miles below the earth. She can't get out until the Prince finds the three –' He hesitated.

'And what, Daddy? The three what?'

'The three – Look? There she is again.'

'The three what?'

'The three – the three stones that will release the King and Queen.'

He yawned.

'And what then?'

'Then he can come and tap three times on each window and that will set her free.'

The lady's head emerged from the upper story of the cabinet-maker's.

'He's busy,' she called down. 'Gosh, what a nice day!'

'And what, Daddy?' asked the little girl. 'Why does the Ogre want to keep her there?'

'Because he wasn't invited to the christening. The Prince has already found one stone in President Coolidge's collar-box. He's looking for the second in Iceland. Every time he finds a stone the room where the Princess is kept turns blue. *Gosh*!' 50

'What Daddy?'

'Just as you turned away I could see the room turn blue. That means he's found the second stone.' 55

'Gosh!' said the little girl. 'Look! It turned blue again, that means he's found the third stone.'

Aroused by the competition the man looked around cautiously and his voice grew tense. 60

'Do you see what I see?' he demanded. 'Coming up the street – there's the Ogre himself, disguised – you know: transformed, like *Mombi* in "The Land of Oz." '

'I know.'

They both watched. The small boy, extraordinarily small and taking very long steps, went to the door of the flat and knocked; no one answered but he didn't seem to expect it or to be greatly disappointed. He took some chalk from his pocket and began drawing pictures under the door-bell. 65

'He's making magic signs,' whispered the man. 'He wants to be sure that the Princess doesn't get out this door. He must know that the Prince has set the King and Queen free and will be along for her pretty soon.' 70

The small boy lingered for a moment; then he went to a window and called an unintelligible word. After a while a woman threw the window open and made an answer that the crisp wind blew away. 75

'She says she's got the Princess locked up,' explained the man.

'Look at the Ogre,' said the little girl. 'He's making magic signs under the window too. And on the sidewalk. Why?'

'He wants to keep her from getting out, of course. That's why he's dancing. That's a charm too — it's a magic dance.' 80

The Ogre went away, taking very big steps. Two men crossed the street ahead and passed out of sight.

How do you think the father is going to include these two men in the story? How do you think he is going to develop the story now?

'Who are they, Daddy?'

'They're two of the King's soldiers. I think the army must be gathering over on Market Street to surround the house. Do you know what "surround" means?' 85

'Yes. Are those men soldiers too?'

'Those too. And I believe that the old one just behind is the King himself. He's keeping bent down low like that so that the Ogre's people won't recognize him.' 90

'Who is the lady?'

'She's a Witch, a friend of the Ogre's.'

The shutter blew closed with a bang and then slowly opened again.

'That's done by the good and bad fairies,' the man explained. 'They're invisible, but the bad fairies want to close the shutter so nobody can see in and the good ones want to open it.'

'The good fairies are winning now.'

'Yes.' He looked at the little girl. 'You're my good fairy.'

'Yes. Look, Daddy! What is that man?'

'He's in the King's army too.' The clerk of Mr. Miller, the jeweller, went by with a somewhat unmartial aspect. 'Hear the whistle? That means they're gathering. And listen – there goes the drum.'

'There's the Queen, Daddy. Look at there. Is that the Queen?'

'No, that's a girl called Miss Television.' He yawned. He began to think of something pleasant that had happened yesterday. He went into a trance. Then he looked at the little girl and saw that she was quite happy. She was six and lovely to look at. He kissed her.

'That man carrying the cake of ice is also one of the King's soldiers,' he said. 'He's going to put the ice on the Ogre's head and freeze his brains so he can't do any more harm.'

Her eyes followed the man down the street. Other men passed. A darky in a yellow darky's overcoat drove by with a cart marked The Del Upholstery Co. The shutter banged again and then slowly opened.

'See, Daddy, the good fairies are winning again.'

The man was old enough to know that he would look back to that time – the tranquil street and the pleasant weather and the mystery playing before the child's eyes, mystery which he had created, but whose luster and texture he could never see or touch any more himself. Again he touched his daughter's cheek instead and in payment fitted another small boy and limping man into the story.

'Oh, I love you,' he said.

'I know, Daddy,' she answered, abstractedly. She was staring at the house. For a moment he closed his eyes and tried to see with her but he couldn't see – those ragged blinds were drawn against him forever. There were only the occasional darkies and the small boys and the weather that reminded him of more glamorous mornings in the past.

The lady came out of the cabinet-maker's shop.

'How did it go?' he asked.

'Good. Il dit qu'il a fait les maisons de poupée pour les Du Ponts. Il va le faire.'

'Combien?'

'Vingt-cinq. I'm sorry I was so long.'

'Look, Daddy, there go a lot more soldiers!'

They drove off. When they had gone a few miles the man turned around and said, 'We saw the most remarkable thing while you were there.' He summarized the episode. 'It's too bad we couldn't wait and see the rescue.'

'But we did,' the child cried. 'They had the rescue in the next street. And there's the Ogre's body in that yard there. The King and Queen and Prince were killed and now the Princess is Queen.' 140

He had liked his King and Queen and felt that they had been too summarily disposed of.

'You had to have a heroine,' he said rather impatiently.

'She'll marry somebody and make him Prince.'

They rode on abstractedly. The lady thought about the doll's house, 145 for she had been poor and had never had one as a child, the man thought how he had almost a million dollars and the little girl thought about the odd doings on the dingy street that they had left behind.

See Glossary section at the back of the book for vocabulary.

First reaction

12 Try to put into words the feelings the three characters have as they drive away.

Close reading

Interpreting characters' motivation

13 Three different ways of finishing the following sentences are given below. Which seems most likely in each case?

a) The man and woman speak in French (lines 9-10, 13, 129-32)
  i) because they don't want the little girl to understand what they are talking about.
  ii) because they are French.
  iii) because they once lived in France.

b) 'I love you too,' said the little girl, smiling politely (line 21). The word 'politely' is used
  i) because she is speaking to a stranger, and so she is formal and polite.
  ii) because she doesn't feel any particularly strong emotion at that moment, but still wants to please the man.
  iii) because she is a very polite girl; so, she always speaks politely.

c) 'Aroused by the competition' (line 59) means that
  i) the man is excited by the room turning blue again.
  ii) the man becomes more interested in telling the story because the little girl is participating too.
  iii) the man feels that the little girl is challenging him.

d) The small boy in lines 61-82
  i) is a friend of a son or daughter of the woman in the flat.

ii) is a complete stranger; nobody in the flat knows him.
iii) works for a local shop.

e) 'No, that's a girl called Miss Television.' (line 104) The man uses the word 'television', which is not traditionally a part of fairy stories, because
i) he is rather tired of the story now, and his concentration is beginning to lapse.
ii) he thinks the little girl is getting tired of the story, so he tries to think of an interesting new element to get her attention back.
iii) he wants to bring the traditional form of the fairy story up to date.

f) Look at lines 115-26. The real reason the man is telling the story is
i) because he wants to recapture his lost childhood.
ii) because he is an artist.
iii) to please the little girl, whom he loves.

g) The man is
i) a generous millionaire.
ii) rich now, but he was once poor.
iii) rich, partly because he is careful with money.

14 An interesting effect comes from the way Fitzgerald makes reality and fiction co-operate with each other.

a) The man is a good story-teller and is very good at improvising – he is able to fit what happens in reality into the story he is making up. We see the first example of this at lines 23-6 where the man notices that the room is obscured by curtains and shutters. After this observation he builds up the idea that something mysterious is going on in the room. Find some other examples of the man's ability to convert what happens in the street into events or characters in the story that he is making up.
b) There are two moments in Fitzgerald's story where what happens in reality is very convenient for the story that the man is making up. The first is at lines 32-3: just *after* the man has said that the princess has golden hair, part of a yellow dress appears momentarily, looking like the princess's hair. If the dress had been black, or green with orange stripes, or any other colour, it might have been more difficult to fit into the story! Find the other moment where reality seems to behave conveniently, and fits in with the story that the man is making up.

Language practice

Speculating about past events (Conditional sentences type 3) *if* + past perfect tense, . . . *would/might have* + past participle

15 Let's imagine that events in the street had been different – how do you think the man would have fitted them into the story?

Example: (lines 31-3) 'If part of a brown dress had appeared in the window . . .'

If part of a brown dress had appeared in the window the man *would* have said it was one of the Ogre's guards.
If part of the brown dress had appeared in the window the man *might* have said it was one of the Princess's servants.

a) (lines 66-7) If the little boy had been let into the flat . . .
b) (lines 73-5) If the father and daughter had heard the boy say 'Is Johnny in?' and the woman reply 'No, he's in the park.' . . .
c) (line 93) If the shutter had blown closed and stayed closed . . .
d) (lines 108-10) If the man had been carrying a big box marked FRAGILE . . .
e) (lines 111-13) If the little girl had asked about the Del Upholstery company van . . .

16 Challenge your powers of improvisation (or that of other students) by asking and answering the questions about what the man would have said if other things had happened. Use the following ideas and then make up some of your own.

Example: if/shutter/fall off . . .

What *would* the father have said if a shutter had fallen off?
He *would/might* have said that the good fairies had won the battle against the bad fairies.

a) if/fire engine/come down the street?
b) if/woman/come out of the flat?
c) if/police patrol/walk past?
d) if/group of children/start playing outside the flat?
e) if/small boy say . . .?
f) if/. . .?

Vocabulary

Reporting verbs; adverbs with direct speech

17 Scott Fitzgerald often uses simply 'he said' or 'she said' after direct speech, but occasionally he gives us a clearer idea of how his characters speak. Here are some examples:

What was said	How it was said		
	Reporting verb	*Adverb*	*Extra Detail*
[l. 70] 'He's making magic signs'	whispered		
[l. 122] 'I know, Daddy'		abstractedly	
[l. 61] 'Do you see what I see?'			looked around cautiously and his voice grew tense

From the following collection of verbs and adverbs, can you say which adverbs could go with which verbs? Use your dictionary if necessary. Make a list of what combinations are possible. For example, you will probably decide that *yawn sleepily* and *yawn loudly* are possible combinations, while *shout abstractedly* is not possible. Is *whisper loudly* ever a possible combination?

Verbs

hesitate scream mutter sneer exclaim whisper explain
yawn shout grumble stutter sigh call

Adverbs

uncertainly politely sleepily inaudibly mockingly abstractedly
impatiently loudly romantically complainingly patiently
softly sarcastically lovingly menacingly

18 Group work

Choose some of the following sentences and after them write a reporting verb and an adverb. Give them to another student, who should speak the sentences according to your description of how they are said, so that the rest of the group will be able to guess the verbs and adverbs you used.

I love you, Daddy
Where have you been?
This could only happen to me.
Never again.
Well, I never knew that.
Good morning!

Example: 'I love you, Daddy,' she whispered lovingly.
'Never again,' she shouted impatiently.

Extension

19 Discussion
Fitzgerald's title is – perhaps deliberately – neutral. From the list below choose the title that best, in your opinion, describes this short story, or invent a title yourself.

The Doll's House	Innocence and Experience
The Princess and the Ogre	Money Can't Buy Everything
A Fairy Tale of New York	In Search of Lost Time
Those Ragged Blinds	Father and Daughter
The World of Imagination	Once Upon a Time

Your title ______________________________

20 What is the attraction of fairy tales?

21 Which story did you prefer, Wilde's or Fitzgerald's? Why?

22 Composition
Write a fairy tale in a modern setting that leads up to the moral: Every cloud has a silver lining, or Never count your chickens until they are hatched. (about 200 words)

23 Write a favourite traditional fairy tale from your country (about 200 words)

Beyond the text

A modern version of a fairy story

24 Here is a version of the famous European fairy tale, *Red Riding Hood,* as rewritten by the American humorist James Thurber in 1939 as *The Little Girl and the Wolf.* Fill in the numbered gaps with **one** suitable word.

One afternoon a big wolf waited in a forest (**1**) ______ a little girl to come along (**2**) ______ a basket of food to her grandmother. (**3**) ______ a little girl did come along (**4**) ______ she was carrying a basket of food. 'Are you carrying that basket to your grandmother?' (**5**) ______ the wolf. The little girl says yes, she was. So the wolf asked her where (**6**) ______ grandmother lived and the little girl

(**7**) ______ him and he disappeared into the (**8**) ______. When the little girl opened the (**9**) ______ of her grandmother's house she saw (**10**) ______ there was somebody in bed with a nightcap (**11**) ______. She had approached no nearer (**12**) ______ twenty-five feet from the bed when she (**13**) ______ that it was not her grandmother but a (**14**) ______, for even in a nightcap a wolf (**15**) ______ not look any more like your (**16**) ______ than the Metro-Goldwyn lion looks like Calvin Coolidge. (**17**) ______ the little girl took an automatic (**18**) ______ of her basket and shot the wolf dead.

Moral: it is not (**19**) ______ easy to fool little girls nowadays as it used to be.

Vocabulary

says: *sometimes in colloquial story-telling the present tense is used instead of the past tense*
The Metro-Goldwyn-Mayer lion: *the logo of the MGM motion picture company; it is the lion that you see roaring on the screen before the beginning of films made by MGM.*
Calvin Coolidge: *President of the USA from 1923 to 1929*
automatic: *a pistol*

What are the elements in Thurber's version of this fairy tale that are not traditional?

Authors

Oscar Wilde (1854-1900) was born in Dublin, Ireland and studied at Dublin and Oxford Universities. He married in 1884. In the 1880s he was a well-known figure on the London literary scene, but in the early 1890s he had a homosexual love affair with Lord Alfred Douglas, causing great scandal and leading to two years' imprisonment for homosexual offences in 1895. He left prison bankrupt, and went to France where he died in 1900.

Wilde is equally well known for his writing as for his brilliant wit and dandyism (his love of aestheticism, his devotion to beauty). He wrote fairy tales for his sons (*The Happy Prince and Other Tales*, 1888, followed by *Lord Arthur Savile's Crime and Other Stories*), and one novel (*The Picture of Dorian Gray*, 1891). Wilde's brilliant verbal wit can be seen in his plays; his masterpiece is *The Importance of Being Earnest*, 1895.

Francis Scott Fitzgerald (1896-1940) was born in Minnesota and educated at Princeton University. He became famous overnight with his first novel, *This Side of Paradise,* (1920), about glamorous student life at Princeton. He then married Zelda Sayre, and they started a life together of high living, party going and big spending. They are seen as representative of the 'Jazz Age', that period enjoyed by rich young Americans in the 1920s. His novels *The Beautiful and The Damned,* (1922), and *The Great Gatsby,* (1925), (his most famous, filmed by Jack Clayton, with Robert Redford and Mia Farrow) are set in this atmosphere, where fragility and unhappiness are always just below the glittering surface. In the 1930s Zelda had a nervous breakdown and Fitzgerald started drinking heavily. *Tender is the Night* (1934), set among rich Americans on the French Riviera, records the end of the Jazz Age. After a nervous breakdown himself, Fitzgerald spent his last few years working as a scriptwriter in Hollywood, where he died of a heart attack. His short stories are *Flappers and Philosophers* (1920), *Tales of the Jazz Age* (1922), *All the Sad Young Men* (1925) and *Taps at Reveille* (1935).

6 Whodunnit?

LAMB TO THE SLAUGHTER
Roald Dahl

Before you read

1 What would be the ingredients of 'the perfect murder'? Put the following ideas into order of importance. Add ideas of your own if you want to.

a) It should be easy to arrange.
b) It should leave no clues.
c) There should be no noise.
d) It should look like suicide.
e) It should take place in a lonely, isolated place.
f) It should be cheap.
g) No violence should be necessary.
h) It should look like an accident.
i) It should be quick.
j) The murderer should have a good alibi.

1) — 2) — 3) — 4) — 5) — 6) — 7) — 8) — 9) —10) —

Lamb to the Slaughter

The room was warm and clean, the curtains drawn, the two table lamps alight – hers and the one by the empty chair opposite. On the sideboard behind her, two tall glasses, soda water, whisky. Fresh ice cubes in the Thermos bucket.

Mary Maloney was waiting for her husband to come home from work. 5

Now and again she would glance up at the clock, but without anxiety, merely to please herself with the thought that each minute gone by made it nearer the time when he would come. There was a slow smiling air about her, and about everything she did. The drop of the head as she bent over her sewing was curiously tranquil. Her skin – for this was her 10 sixth month with child – had acquired a wonderful translucent quality, the mouth was soft, and the eyes, with their new placid look, seemed larger, darker than before.

When the clock said ten minutes to five, she began to listen, and a few moments later, punctually as always, she heard the tyres on the gravel 15 outside, and the car door slamming, the footsteps passing the window, the key turning in the lock. She laid aside her sewing, stood up, and went forward to kiss him as he came in.

What does this description of Mary Maloney waiting for her husband tell us about her feelings towards him?

'Hullo, darling,' she said.

'Hullo,' he answered.

She took his coat and hung it in the closet. Then she walked over and made the drinks, a strongish one for him, a weak one for herself; and soon she was back again in her chair with the sewing, and he in the other, opposite, holding the tall glass with both his hands, rocking it so the ice cubes tinkled against the side.

For her, this was always a blissful time of day. She knew he didn't want to speak much until the first drink was finished, and she, on her side, was content to sit quietly, enjoying his company after the long hours alone in the house. She loved to luxuriate in the presence of this man, and to feel – almost as a sunbather feels the sun – that warm male glow that came out of him to her when they were alone together. She loved him for the way he sat loosely in a chair, for the way he came in a door, or moved slowly across the room with long strides. She loved the intent, far look in his eyes when they rested on her, the funny shape of the mouth, and especially the way he remained silent about his tiredness, sitting still with himself until the whisky had taken some of it away.

'Tired, darling?'

'Yes' he said. 'I'm tired.' And as he spoke, he did an unusual thing. He lifted his glass and drained it in one swallow although there was still half of it, at least half of it, left. She wasn't really watching him but she knew what he had done because she heard the ice cubes falling back against the bottom of the empty glass when he lowered his arm. He paused a moment, leaning forward in the chair, then he got up and went slowly over to fetch himself another.

'I'll get it!' she cried, jumping up.

'Sit down,' he said.

When he came back, she noticed that the new drink was dark amber with the quantity of whisky in it.

'Darling, shall I get your slippers?'

'No.'

She watched him as he began to sip the dark yellow drink, and she could see little oily swirls in the liquid because it was so strong.

'I think it's a shame,' she said, 'that when a policeman gets to be as senior as you, they keep him walking about on his feet all day long.'

He didn't answer, so she bent her head again and went on with her sewing; but each time he lifted the drink to his lips, she heard the ice cubes clinking against the side of the glass.

'Darling,' she said. 'Would you like me to get you some cheese? I haven't made any supper because it's Thursday.'

'No,' he said.

'If you're too tired to eat out,' she went on, 'it's still not too late. There's plenty of meat and stuff in the freezer, and you can have it right here and not even move out of the chair.'

Her eyes waited on him for an answer, a smile, a little nod, but he made no sign.

'Anyway,' she went on, 'I'll get you some cheese and crackers first.'

'I don't want it,' he said.

She moved uneasily in her chair, the large eyes still watching his face. 'But you *must* have supper. I can easily do it here. I'd like to do it. We can have lamb chops. Or pork. Anything you want. Everything's in the freezer.'

'Forget it,' he said.

'But, darling, you *must* eat! I'll fix it anyway, and then you can have it or not, as you like.'

She stood up and placed her sewing on the table by the lamp.

'Sit down,' he said. 'Just for a minute, sit down.'

It wasn't till then that she began to get frightened.

'Go on,' he said. 'Sit down.'

> *Can you think of any explanations for his strange behaviour?*

She lowered herself back slowly into the chair, watching him all the time with those large, bewildered eyes. He had finished the second drink and was staring down into the glass, frowning.

'Listen,' he said. 'I've got something to tell you.'

'What is it, darling? What's the matter?'

He had become absolutely motionless, and he kept his head down so that the light from the lamp beside him fell across the upper part of his face, leaving the chin and mouth in shadow. She noticed there was a little muscle moving near the corner of his left eye.

'This is going to be a bit of a shock to you, I'm afraid,' he said. 'But I've thought about it a good deal and I've decided the only thing to do is tell you right away. I hope you won't blame me too much.'

And he told her. It didn't take long, four or five minutes at most, and she sat very still through it all, watching him with a kind of dazed horror as he went further and further away from her with each word.

'So there it is,' he added. 'And I know it's kind of a bad time to be telling you, but there simply wasn't any other way. Of course I'll give you money and see you're looked after. But there needn't really be any fuss. I hope not anyway. It wouldn't be very good for my job.'

Her first instinct was not to believe any of it, to reject it all. It occurred to her that perhaps he hadn't even spoken, that she herself had imagined the whole thing. Maybe, if she went about her business and acted as though she hadn't been listening, then later, when she sort of woke up again, she might find none of it had ever happened.

'I'll get the supper,' she managed to whisper, and this time he didn't stop her.

> *What exactly has he told her, do you think?*

When she walked across the room she couldn't feel her feet touching the floor. She couldn't feel anything at all – except a slight nausea and a desire to vomit. Everything was automatic now – down the stairs to the cellar, the light switch, the deep freeze, the hand inside the cabinet taking hold of the first object it met. She lifted it out, and looked at it. It was wrapped in paper, so she took off the paper and looked at it again.

A leg of lamb.

All right then, they would have lamb for supper. She carried it upstairs, holding the thin bone-end of it with both her hands, and as she went through the living-room, she saw him standing over by the window with his back to her, and she stopped.

'For God's sake,' he said, hearing her, but not turning round. 'Don't make supper for me. I'm going out.'

At that point, Mary Maloney simply walked up behind him and without any pause she swung the big frozen leg of lamb high in the air and brought it down as hard as she could on the back of his head.

She might just as well have hit him with a steel club.

She stepped back a pace, waiting, and the funny thing was that he remained standing there for at least four or five seconds, gently swaying. Then he crashed to the carpet.

The violence of the crash, the noise, the small table overturning, helped bring her out of the shock. She came out slowly, feeling cold and surprised, and she stood for a while blinking at the body, still holding the ridiculous piece of meat tight with both hands.

All right, she told herself. So I've killed him.

It was extraordinary, now, how clear her mind became all of a sudden. She began thinking very fast. As the wife of a detective, she knew quite well what the penalty would be. That was fine. It made no difference to her. In fact, it would be a relief. On the other hand, what about the child? What were the laws about murderers with unborn children? Did they kill them both – mother and child? Or did they wait until the tenth month? What did they do?

Mary Maloney didn't know. And she certainly wasn't prepared to take a chance.

She carried the meat into the kitchen, placed it in a pan, turned the oven on high, and shoved it inside. Then she washed her hands and ran upstairs to the bedroom. She sat down before the mirror, tidied her face, touched up her lips and face. She tried a smile. It came out rather peculiar. She tried again.

'Hullo Sam,' she said brightly, aloud.

The voice sounded peculiar too.

'I want some potatoes please, Sam. Yes, and I think a can of peas.'

That was better. Both the smile and the voice were coming out better now. She rehearsed it several times more. Then she ran downstairs, took her coat, went out the back door, down the garden, into the street.

What do you think she is going to do? Do you think she has some kind of plan?

It wasn't six o'clock yet and the lights were still on in the grocery shop.

'Hullo Sam,' she said brightly, smiling at the man behind the counter.
'Why, good evening, Mrs Maloney. How're *you*?'

'I want some potatoes please, Sam. Yes, and I think a can of peas.' 155

The man turned and reached up behind him on the shelf for the peas.

'Patrick's decided he's tired and doesn't want to eat out tonight,' she told him. 'We usually go out Thursdays, you know, and now he's caught me without any vegetables in the house.'

'Then how about meat, Mrs Maloney?' 160

'No, I've got meat, thanks. I got a nice leg of lamb, from the freezer.'

'Oh.'

'I don't much like cooking it frozen, Sam, but I'm taking a chance on it this time. You think it'll be all right?'

'Personally,' the grocer said, 'I don't believe it makes any difference. 165 You want these Idaho potatoes?'

'Oh yes, that'll be fine. Two of those.'

'Anything else?' The grocer cocked his head on one side, looking at her pleasantly. 'How about afterwards? What you going to give him for afterwards?' 170

'Well – what would you suggest, Sam?'

The man glanced around his shop. 'How about a nice big slice of cheesecake? I know he likes that.'

'Perfect,' she said. 'He loves it.'

And when it was all wrapped and she had paid, she put on her 175 brightest smile and said, 'Thank you, Sam. Good night.'

'Good night, Mrs Maloney. And thank *you*.'

And now, she told herself as she hurried back, all she was doing now, she was returning home to her husband and he was waiting for his supper; and she must cook it good, and make it as tasty as possible 180 because the poor man was tired; and if, when she entered the house, she happened to find anything unusual, or tragic, or terrible, then naturally it would be a shock and she'd become frantic with grief and horror. Mind you, she wasn't *expecting* to find anything. She was just going home with the vegetables. Mrs Patrick Maloney going home with 185 the vegetables on Thursday evening to cook supper for her husband.

That's the way, she told herself. Do everything right and natural. Keep things absolutely natural and there'll be no need for any acting at all.

Therefore, when she entered the kitchen by the back door, she was 190 humming a little tune to herself and smiling.

'Patrick!' she called. 'How are you, darling?'

She put the parcel down on the table and went through into the living-room; and when she saw him lying there on the floor with his legs doubled up and one arm twisted back underneath his body, it really was 195 rather a shock. All the old love and longing for him welled up inside her, and she ran over to him, knelt down beside him, and began to cry her heart out. It was easy. No acting was necessary.

A few minutes later she got up and went to the phone. She knew the number of the police station, and when the man at the other end 200 answered, she cried to him, 'Quick! Come quick! Patrick's dead!'

'Who's speaking?'

'Mrs Maloney. Mrs Patrick Maloney.'

'You mean Patrick Maloney's dead?'

'I think so,' she sobbed. 'He's lying on the floor and I think he's dead.' 205

'Be right over,' the man said.

The car came very quickly, and when she opened the front door, two policemen walked in. She knew them both – she knew nearly all the men at that precinct – and she fell right into Jack Noonan's arms, weeping hysterically. He put her gently into a chair, then went over to 210 join the other one, who was called O'Malley, kneeling by the body.

'Is he dead?' she cried.

'I'm afraid he is. What happened?'

Briefly, she told her story about going out to the grocer and coming back to find him on the floor. While she was talking, crying and talking, 215 Noonan discovered a small patch of congealed blood on the dead man's head. He showed it to O'Malley who got up at once and hurried to the phone.

What will the police think? Do you think they will suspect Mary?

Soon, other men began to come into the house. First a doctor, then two detectives, one of whom she knew by name. Later, a police 220 photographer arrived and took pictures, and a man who knew about fingerprints. There was a great deal of whispering and muttering beside the corpse, and the detectives kept asking her a lot of questions. But they always treated her kindly. She told her story again, this time right from the beginning, when Patrick had come in, and she was sewing, 225 and he was tired, so tired he hadn't wanted to go out for supper. She told how she'd put the meat in the oven – 'it's there now, cooking' – and how she'd slipped out to the grocer for vegetables, and come back to find him lying on the floor.

'Which grocer?' one of the detectives asked. 230

She told him, and he turned and whispered something to the other detective who immediately went outside into the street.

In fifteen minutes he was back with a page of notes, and there was more whispering, and through her sobbing she heard a few of the whispered phrases – '. . . acted quite normal . . . very cheerful . . . 235 wanted to give him a good supper . . . peas . . . cheesecake . . . impossible that she . . .'

After a while, the photographer and the doctor departed and two other men came in and took the corpse away on a stretcher. Then the fingerprint man went away. The two detectives remained, and so did 240 the two policemen. They were exceptionally nice to her, and Jack Noonan asked if she wouldn't rather go somewhere else, to her sister's house perhaps, or to his own wife who would take care of her and put her up for the night.

No, she said. She didn't feel she could move even a yard at the 245 moment. Would they mind awfully if she stayed just where she was until she felt better? She didn't feel too good at the moment, she really didn't.

Then hadn't she better lie down on the bed? Jack Noonan asked.

No, she said, she'd like to stay right where she was, in this chair. A little later perhaps, when she felt better, she would move. 250

So they left her there while they went about their business, searching the house. Occasionally one of the detectives asked her another question. Sometimes Jack Noonan spoke to her gently as he passed by. Her husband, he told her, had been killed by a blow on the back of the head administered with a heavy blunt instrument, almost certainly a large piece of metal. They were looking for the weapon. The murderer may have taken it with him, but on the other hand he may've thrown it away or hidden it somewhere on the premises. 255

'It's the old story,' he said. 'Get the weapon, and you've got the man.' 260

Later, one of the detectives came up and sat beside her. Did she know, he asked, of anything in the house that could've been used as the weapon? Would she mind having a look around to see if anything was missing – a very big spanner, for example, or a heavy metal vase.

They didn't have any heavy metal vases, she said. 265

'Or a big spanner?'

She didn't think they had a big spanner. But there might be some things like that in the garage.

The search went on. She knew that there were other policemen in the garden all around the house. She could hear their footsteps on the gravel outside, and sometimes she saw the flash of a torch through a chink in the curtains. It began to get late, nearly nine she noticed by the clock on the mantel. The four men searching the rooms seemed to be growing weary, a trifle exasperated. 270

Do you think the police will have any success in their search for the murder weapon?

'Jack, she said, the next time Sergeant Noonan went by. 'Would you mind giving me a drink?' 275

'Sure I'll give you a drink. You mean this whisky?'

'Yes, please. But just a small one. It might make me feel better.'

He handed her the glass.

'Why don't you have one yourself,' she said. 'You must be awfully tired. Please do. You've been very good to me.' 280

'Well,' he answered. 'It's not strictly allowed, but I might take just a drop to keep me going.'

One by one the others came in and were persuaded to take a little nip of whisky. They stood around rather awkwardly with the drinks in their hands, uncomfortable in her presence, trying to say consoling things to her. Sergeant Noonan wandered into the kitchen, came out quickly and said, 'Look, Mrs Maloney. You know that oven of yours is still on, and the meat still inside.' 285

'Oh, *dear* me!' she cried. 'So it is!' 290

'I better turn it off for you, hadn't I?'

'Will you do that, Jack. Thank you so much.'

When the sergeant returned the second time, she looked at him with her large, dark, tearful eyes. 'Jack Noonan,' she said.

'Yes?' 295

'Would you do me a small favour – you and these others?'

'We can try, Mrs Maloney.'

'Well,' she said. 'Here you all are, and good friends of dear Patrick's too, and helping to catch the man who killed him. You must be terrible hungry by now because it's long past your supper time, and I know 300 Patrick would never forgive me, God bless his soul, if I allowed you to remain in his house without offering you decent hospitality. Why don't you eat up that lamb that's in the oven? It'll be cooked just right by now.'

'Wouldn't dream of it,' Sergeant Noonan said. 305

'Please,' she begged. 'Please eat it. Personally I couldn't touch a thing, certainly not what's been in the house when he was here. But it's all right for you. It'd be a favour to me if you'd eat it up. Then you can go on with your work again afterwards.'

There was a good deal of hesitating among the four policemen, but 310 they were clearly hungry, and in the end they were persuaded to go into the kitchen and help themselves. The woman stayed where she was, listening to them through the open door, and she could hear them speaking among themselves, their voices thick and sloppy because their mouths were full of meat. 315

'Have some more, Charlie?'

'No. Better not finish it.'

'She *wants* us to finish it. She said so. Be doing her a favour.'

'Okay then. Give me some more.'

'That's the hell of a big club the guy must've used to hit poor Patrick,' 320 one of them was saying. 'The doc says his skull was smashed all to pieces just like from a sledge-hammer.'

'That's why it ought to be easy to find.'

'Exactly what I say.'

'Whoever done it, they're not going to be carrying a thing like that 325 around with them longer than they need.'

One of them belched.

'Personally, I think it's right here on the premises.'

'Probably right under our very noses. What you think, Jack?'

And in the other room Mary Maloney began to giggle. 330

See Glossary section at the back of the book for vocabulary.

First reaction

2 Which of these comments do you agree with?

a) Mr Maloney gets what he deserved for treating his wife the way he does. This is a moral story with a very satisfactory ending.

b) This is simply a witty, amusing story: morality has got nothing to do with it. Dahl's purpose is to make the reader laugh, not to judge the characters.

c) This story is immoral. At the end Mrs Maloney doesn't show any regret for what she has done. She even seems glad, and it looks as though she isn't going to be found out.

Close reading

Interpreting characters' actions

3 a) The reader is given a number of clues that Mr Maloney is preoccupied by something (lines 19-83). List them.

b) Is there anything that makes the reader think that Mr Maloney is a rather unpleasant man? (lines 19-98)

4 Choose the phrase that best completes the following sentences. Sometimes your choice will depend on evidence in the story, sometimes on your personal interpretation.

a) When Mr Maloney tells his wife something that will be 'a bit of a shock' to her

- **i)** it is the confirmation of something that she has suspected for a long time.
- **ii)** it comes as a complete surprise to her.
- **iii)** it is the confirmation of something that she has suspected ever since he came home that evening.

b) Mary Maloney thinks of killing her husband

- **i)** soon after he finishes speaking to her.
- **ii)** when she finds the leg of lamb in the freezer.
- **iii)** when he says 'For God's sake, don't make supper for me. I'm going out.'
- **iv)** she never thinks of it: she does it unconsciously.

c) When Mary puts the lamb in the oven

- **i)** she has just invented a plan to hide the murder weapon.
- **ii)** she is following the plan she had thought of when she killed her husband.

iii) she does it unconsciously: she would have done this anyway.

d) When Mary sees her husband dead on the floor after she comes back from the shop

i) she is genuinely shocked.
ii) she pretends to be shocked.
iii) she is shocked, even though she knew what to expect.

e) Mary begins to cry when the police arrive because

i) she deeply regrets killing her husband.
ii) she is acting: she thinks this is the reaction the police will expect.
iii) she is terrified of what might happen to her.
iv) she is in a state of shock: she feels a variety of emotions.

f) When Jack Noonan asks her if she would like to spend the night somewhere else, she refuses because

i) she wants to keep an eye on what the policemen are doing.
ii) she is too shocked to move.
iii) she has already thought of the idea of inviting the policemen to eat the lamb.

g) Mary asks for a drink herself, and offers a drink to the policemen because

i) she needs a drink to calm her nerves.
ii) she wants to create a diversion, as the policemen are still looking for the murder weapon.
iii) she feels sorry for the policemen, who are friends of hers.

h) Mary invites them to eat the lamb because

i) she wants to destroy the evidence.
ii) she feels sorry for the policemen, who must be feeling hungry by now.
iii) the lamb reminds her of what she has done, and she can't bear to have it in the house.

i) At the end of the story, Mary giggles because

i) she is rather drunk: she has been drinking whisky on an empty stomach.
ii) the policemen are so stupid.
iii) she feels a mixture of emotions: relief, nervousness, and even an appreciation of the absurdity of the situation.
iv) she is still nervous and worried about being found out.

j) Why does Mary decide not to confess to the murder?

____

5 Look at the dictionary definitions, then choose the interpretation of the title you most agree with. If you think none of the interpretations is satisfactory or sufficient by itself, you can write an interpretation of your own.

lamb /læm/ *n* **1** (**a**) [C] young sheep. ⇨ illus at SHEEP. Cf. EWE. (**b**) [U] its flesh as food: *a leg of lamb* ○ [attrib] *lamb chops*. Cf. MUTTON. **2** (*infml*) gentle or dear person. **3** (idm) **one may might as well be hanged/hung for a sheep as a lamb** ⇨ HANG. **like a lamb (to the slaughter)** without resisting or protesting: *She surprised us all on her first day of school by going off like a lamb.* **mutton dressed as lamb** ⇨ MUTTON.
▷ **lamb** *v* [I] **1** (of a ewe) give birth to lambs: *lambing ewes.* **2** (of a farmer) tend ewes doing this: *the lambing season,* ie when lambs are born.
□ **lambskin** *n* **1** [C] skin of lamb with its wool on (used to make coats, gloves, etc). **2** [U] leather made from this.
lamb's-wool *n* [U] soft fine fluffy wool from lambs, used for making knitted clothes: *a scarf made of lamb's-wool* ○ [attrib] *a lamb's-wool cardigan.*

slaughter /ˈslɔːtə(r)/*n* [U] **1** the killing of animals, esp for food. **2** the killing of many people at once; massacre: *the slaughter of innocent civilians* ○ *the slaughter on the roads,* ie the killing of people in road accidents. **3** (*infml*) complete defeat: *the total slaughter of the home team.*
▷ **slaugh-ter** *v* [Tn] **1** (**a**) kill (an animal), usu for food: *slaughter pigs by humane methods.* (**b**) kill (animals or people) in large numbers: *thousands slaughtered by the invading army.* **2** (*fig infml*) defeat (sb/sth) completely, esp in sport: *We slaughtered them at hockey.*
□ **slaughterhouse** (also **abbatoir**) *n* place where animals are killed for food.

(Oxford Advanced Learner's Dictionary)

a) Mr Maloney has done nothing wrong; or if he has done something wrong he has, at least, acted honestly. He is the innocent lamb in the title who has been slaughtered. It may even be that his wife has always been unbalanced, and he has finally found the courage to leave her.

b) The lamb in the title refers to gentle, harmless Mrs Maloney, who finds herself, because of the circumstances and without any premeditation, killing her husband.

c) The title is a joke: it makes the reader think of a common expression meaning 'death without protest', but its real meaning is that a leg of lamb is used as the murder weapon.

d) The title is ironic. Neither Mr Maloney nor Mrs Maloney is a *lamb* (he is certainly not gentle, she is certainly not obedient), and there is no *slaughter* (only one person is killed).

e) Your interpretation? ______________________________

____

____

Language practice

Explaining motivation – Infinitive of purpose; purpose clauses with *so that* . . .

6 Look at these ways of explaining why people do things.

a) The infinitive of purpose (*to* + base form) is used when the subject of the purpose clause is the same as the subject of the main clause:

Mary takes the paper wrapping off the meat *to see* what kind of meat it is.

b) If the verb in the purpose clause is negative, you have to use *so as not to*:

Jack Noonan and the others treat Mary very kindly *so as not to upset* her more than necessary.

c) If the subject of the purpose clause is different from the subject of the main clause (or if the subject of the main clause is repeated in the purpose clause), you have to use *so that* followed by *will (won't)* or *can (can't)*:

Mary offers to cook dinner for her husband *so that he won't have to* go out.
Mary offers to get some meat out of the freezer *so that they can eat* at home.

Note: When the verb in the main clause is in a past tense there is a change of tense in the verb in the purpose clause. This is explained in 8 below.

7 Complete these sentences. In the spaces put *to, so as not to* or *so that.* Then put the verb in the purpose clause (the one in brackets) in a suitable form.

a) Mary goes to Sam's grocery shop ________________ (create) an alibi.

b) Mary prefers to stay at home rather than go to her sister's ________________ she (keep) an eye on the policemen.

c) On the way back from the shop Mary convinces herself that nothing has happened ________________ her grief (appear) natural.

d) Mary decides not to confess to the murder ________________ ________________ (endanger) her child's life.

e) Mary rehearses her conversation with Sam in the mirror ___

_______________ Sam (notice) anything strange in her behaviour.

f) The police went to find the murder weapon _______________ _______________ they (examine) it for fingerprints.

g) A policeman goes to Sam's grocery shop _______________ _______________ (check) Mary's alibi.

h) Mary asks the policemen to eat the lamb _______________ _______________ the evidence (be) destroyed.

i) The detectives whisper their suspicions to each other _______________ Mary (hear).

j) Mr Maloney wants to avoid any fuss about their separation _______________ (cause) a scandal that would affect his career.

8 Sequence of tenses. If the verb in the main clause is in a past tense, the infinitive of purpose does not change, but a modal verb in the purpose clause changes:

Main clause	Purpose clause
verb in a present tense (eg The detectives whisper so that Mary won't hear.)	*to* or *so as not to* + base form of verb OR *so that* + *will (won't)* or *can (can't)*
verb in a past tense (eg The detectives whispered so that Mary wouldn't hear.)	*to* or *so as not to* + base form of verb OR *so that* + *would (wouldn't)* or *could (couldn't)*

9 a) Match the main clauses in the left hand column with the purpose clauses in the right hand column.

Main clause *What was done*	Purpose clause *The reason for doing it*
1 They used a stolen car for the getaway	a) he wanted to be able to run away quickly if necessary.
2 She asked her best friend to say that they had been to the cinema together	b) they didn't want the police to be able to trace the phone calls.
3 He carefully wiped all the surfaces he had touched	c) she didn't want the shot to be heard.
4 They always telephoned from a public telephone box	d) they didn't want the police to be able to connect the car to them.
5 They had a driver waiting outside in a fast car	e) she wanted to make police think the motive was robbery.
6 She fitted a silencer onto the pistol	f) they didn't want anyone to be able to recognize their faces.
7 They sent a message from the girl recorded on a casette	g) she wanted to have an alibi.
8 He didn't take anything that was exceptionally valuable	h) he didn't want to leave any fingerprints.
9 They put women's tights over their faces	i) they didn't want the police to be able to trace the money.
10 He left the back door open	j) he didn't want to have any difficulty in selling it.
11 She took the dead man's wallet	k) they wanted to be able to make a quick getaway.
12 They asked for the money to be paid in used banknotes of small denomination	l) they wanted her parents to know she was still alive.

1) — 2) — 3) — 4) — 5) — 6) — 7) — 8) — 9) —10) — 11) — 12) —

b) Connect the main clauses in the left hand column with the purpose clauses in the right hand column. Use *to, so as not to* or *so that.*

c) Which of the twelve sentences you have made could refer to the crimes of:
i) murder **ii)** bank robbery **iii)** burglary **iv)** kidnapping?

10 Complete these sentences in at least two different ways.

a) He dyed his hair black and grew a beard ____________

b) They had hidden a microphone in his hotel room ____________

c) They threw drugged meat to the guard dogs ____________

d) ____________ so that they wouldn't suspect her.
e) ____________ so as not to look suspicious.
f) ____________ so that nobody would know what had happened.

Vocabulary

Feelings and reactions

11 Mary Maloney, and the policemen who come to investigate, experience a variety of feelings and reactions during the story. Complete the table below. The first two have been done for you. Use your dictionary if necessary. (The words in **a-f** come from the story.)

Noun	Verb	Adjective(s)	
a) anxiety	(no derivative exists) (use: to make someone anxious)	anxious	(no derivative exists)
b) bewilderment	bewilder	bewildered,	bewildering
c) horror	____________	____________,	____________
d) shock	____________	____________,	____________
e) ____________	____________	surprised,	____________
f) ____________	____________	exasperated,	____________
g) ____________	satisfy	____________,	____________
h) worry	____________	____________,	____________
i) ____________	____________	fascinated,	____________
j) ____________	____________	____________,	pleasant/(pleasing)
k) ____________	annoy	____________,	____________
l) amusement	____________	____________,	____________
m) ____________	____________	____________,	outrageous
n) ____________	frighten	____________,	____________
o) charm	____________	____________,	____________
p) ____________	____________	____________,	embarrassing
q) ____________	____________	frustrated,	____________
r) ____________	delight	____________,	____________
s) ____________	____________	____________,	disappointing
t) ____________	____________	disgusted,	____________

12 What connections can you make between the words above? Try to group them in the following ways:

a) words describing pleasant feelings and reactions
b) words describing unpleasant feelings and reactions
c) words describing feelings and reactions that you often experience
d) words describing feelings and reactions that you rarely experience

13 Group work
Discuss these questions in pairs or groups. Then prepare similar questions for other pairs or groups.

What are you frightened of?
What is the most embarrassing thing that has ever happened to you (that you can talk about!)?
What is the most pleasant surprise you have ever had?
What is the most unpleasant surprise you have ever had?
What kinds of things make you anxious?
What kinds of things exasperate you?
What kinds of people do you find fascinating?

Extension

14 Discussion
Do you think thrillers and crime stories are simply for entertainment, or can they teach us something about human nature?

15 Composition
The next day, Mary Maloney decides that she has to confess, but she can't do it face to face with a policeman whom she knows and who knew her husband. Write the letter of confession she gives in at the police station. (about 150-200 words)

Beyond the text

The technique of Sherlock Holmes
16 Perhaps the most famous detective in the world, Sherlock Holmes, was the creation of Arthur Conan Doyle (1859-1930). The Sherlock Holmes stories were an instant success, and so successful were they that when Conan Doyle had Holmes

killed in one of his stories, public demand obliged him to bring Holmes back to life in another series of short stories. Sherlock Holmes' cases can be found in the short novel *The Hound of the Baskervilles,* and in the stories collected in *The Memoirs of Sherlock Holmes, The Case-Book of Sherlock Holmes,* and *The Adventures of Sherlock Holmes.*

Conan Doyle, like Holmes' assistant Dr Watson, was a doctor, and it is said that the methods of diagnosis used by a professor of medicine at Edinburgh University when Conan Doyle was a student there gave him the idea for Holmes' techniques of deduction.

In this extract from the story *The Sign of Four,* we see Dr Watson asking Holmes for a demonstration of his technique. Dr Watson speaks first. Read the extract and fill in the missing words given in the box.

impulse	know	simplicity	remains	observation
send	rest	deduction	avoid	explanation

The Sign of Four

'But you spoke just now of observation and deduction. Surely the one to some extent implies the other.'

'Why, hardly,' he answered, leaning back luxuriously in his armchair and sending up thick blue wreaths from his pipe. 'For example, **(1)** ______________ shows me that you have been to the Wigmore Street Post-Office this morning, but **(2)** ______________ lets me know that when there you dispatched a telegram.'

'Right!' said I. 'Right on both points! But I confess that I don't see how you arrived at it. It was a sudden **(3)** ______________ upon my part, and I have mentioned it to no one.'

'It is **(4)** ______________ itself,' he remarked, chuckling at my surprise – 'so absurdly simple that an **(5)** ______________ is superfluous; and yet it may serve to define the limits of observation and of deduction. Observation tells me that you have a little reddish mould adhering to your instep. Just opposite the Wigmore Street Office they have taken up the pavement and thrown up some earth, which lies in such a way that it is difficult to **(6)** ______________ treading in it in entering. The earth is of this peculiar reddish tint which is found, as far as I **(7)**, ______________ nowhere else in the neighbourhood. So much is observation. The **(8)** ______________ is deduction.'

'How, then, did you deduce the telegram?'

'Why, of course I knew that you had not written a letter, since I sat opposite to you all morning. I see also in your open desk there that you have a sheet of stamps and a thick bundle of postcards. What could you

go into the post-office for, then, but to (**9**) ______________ a wire? 25
Eliminate all other factors, and the one which (**10**) ______________ must be the truth.'

Vocabulary

4 wreaths: *rings of smoke*
7 dispatch: *to send*
11 chuckle: *to laugh quietly*
14 reddish: *of a kind of red colour*
14 mould: *mud, wet earth*
14 adhere: *to stick*
15 instep: *middle part of shoe*
17 tread: *step, put one's foot*
18 tint: *colour*
24 sheet: *page*
24 bundle: *pack*
25 wire: *telegram*

17 Imagine that Sherlock Holmes has been requested to help solve Patrick Maloney's murder. Write a brief account of, or discuss, how he solves the mystery.

Author

Roald Dahl (1916-1990) was born and brought up in Great Britain, though his parents were Norwegian. During the Second World War he was a fighter pilot, and was sent to Washington, where he started writing short stories. Dahl's writing career was extraordinary in that he was famous for writing both for adults and for children. His books for children are distinguished by the fact that they include really unpleasant characters. Some of these stories are *James and the Giant Peach*, *Charlie and the Chocolate Factory* (filmed as *Willie Wonka's Chocolate Factory*, with Gene Wilder), and *The BFG*. He scripted the children's film *Chitty Chitty Bang Bang* about a magical car.

His short stories for adults, in collections such as *Kiss Kiss*, *Switch Bitch* and *Someone Like You* (from which *Lamb To The Slaughter* is taken), are notable for their 'blackness' as well as 'the sting in the tail' or the 'twist' at the end of the story: a very unexpected development which takes the reader by surprise.

He also wrote two volumes of autobiography, *Boy* and *Going Solo*.

7 The Sporting Life

ACE IN THE HOLE
John Updike

Before you read

1 What happens to sports stars when they retire from sporting life? How do you think they cope with the transition into 'ordinary' life?

Ace in the Hole

No sooner did his car touch the boulevard heading home than Ace flicked on the radio. He needed the radio, especially today. In the seconds before the tubes warmed up, he said aloud, doing it just to hear a human voice, 'Jesus. She'll pop her lid.' His voice, though familiar, irked him; it sounded thin and scratchy, as if the bones in his head were picking up static. In a deeper register Ace added, 'She'll murder me.' Then the radio came on, warm and strong, so he stopped worrying. The Five Kings were doing 'Blueberry Hill'; to hear them made Ace feel so sure inside that from the pack pinched between the car roof and the sun shield he plucked a cigarette, hung it on his lower lip, snapped a match across the rusty place on the dash, held the flame in the instinctive spot near the tip of his nose, dragged, and blew out the match, all in time to the music. He rolled down the window and snapped the match so it spun end-over-end into the gutter. 'Two points,' he said, and cocked the cigarette toward the roof of the car, sucked powerfully and exhaled two plumes through his nostrils. He was beginning to feel like himself, Ace Anderson, for the first time that whole day, a bad day. He beat time on the accelerator. The car jerked crazily. 'On Blueberry Hill,' he sang, 'my heart stood still. The wind in the wil-low tree' – he braked for a red light – 'played love's suh-*weet* melodee –'

'Go, Dad, bust your lungs!' a kid's voice blared. The kid was riding in a '52 Pontiac that had pulled up beside Ace at the light. The profile of the driver, another kid, was dark over his shoulder.

Ace looked over at him and smiled slowly, just letting one side of his mouth lift a little. 'Shove it,' he said, good-naturedly, across the little gap of years that separated them. He knew how they felt, young and mean and shy.

But the kid, who looked Greek, lifted his thick upper lip and spat out the window. The spit gleamed on the asphalt like a half-dollar.

'Now isn't that pretty?' Ace said, keeping one eye on the light. 'You miserable wop. You are *mis*erable.' While the kid was trying to think of some smart comeback, the light changed. Ace dug out so hard he smelled burned rubber. In his rear-view mirror he saw the Pontiac lurch forward a few yards, then stop dead, right in the middle of the intersection.

The idea of them stalling their fat tin Pontiac kept him in a good humor all the way home. He decided to stop at his mother's place and pick up the baby, instead of waiting for Evey to do it. His mother must have seen him drive up. She came out on the porch holding a plastic spoon and smelling of cake.

'You're out early,' she told him.

'Friedman fired me,' Ace told her.

'Good for you,' his mother said. 'I always said he never treated you right.' She brought a cigarette out of her apron pocket and tucked it deep into one corner of her mouth, the way she did when something pleased her.

Ace lighted it for her. 'Friedman was O.K. personally,' he said. 'He just wanted too much for his money. I didn't mind working Saturdays, but until eleven, twelve Friday nights was too much. Everybody has a right to some leisure.'

'Well, I don't dare think what Evey will say, but I, for one, thank dear God you had the brains to get out of it. I always said that job had no future to it – no future of any kind, Freddy.'

'I guess,' Ace admitted. 'But I wanted to keep at it, for the family's sake.'

'Now, I know I shouldn't be saying this, but any time Evey – this is just between us – any time Evey thinks she can do better, there's room for you *and* Bonnie right in your father's house.' She pinched her lips together. He could almost hear the old lady think, *There, I've said it*.

'Look, Mom, Evey tries awfully hard, and anyway you know she can't work that way. Not that *that* – I mean, she's a realist, too . . .' He let the rest of the thought fade as he watched a kid across the street dribbling a basketball around a telephone pole that had a backboard and net nailed on it.

'Evey's a wonderful girl of her own kind. But I've always said, and your father agrees, Roman Catholics ought to marry among themselves. Now I know I've said it before, but when they get out in the greater world –'

'*No*, Mom.'

> *What has this conversation told us about the relationships between Ace, his wife (Evey), and his mother? Answer briefly.*

She frowned, smoothed herself, and said, 'Your name was in the paper today.'

Ace chose to let that go by. He kept watching the kid with the basketball. It was funny how, though the whole point was to get the ball up into the air, kids grabbed it by the sides and squeezed. Kids just didn't think.

'Did you hear?' his mother said.

'Sure, but so what?' Ace said. His mother's lower lip was coming at him, so he changed the subject. 'I guess I'll take Bonnie.'

His mother went into the house and brought back his daughter, wrapped in a blue blanket. The baby looked dopey. 'She fussed all day,' 80 his mother complained. 'I said to your father, "Bonnie is a dear little girl, but without a doubt she's her mother's daughter." You were the best-natured boy.'

'Well I *had* everything,' Ace said with an impatience that made his mother blink. He nicely dropped his cigarette into a brown flowerpot on 85 the edge of the porch and took his daughter into his arms. She was getting heavier, solid. When he reached the end of the cement walk, his mother was still on the porch, waving to him. He was so close he could see the fat around her elbow jiggle, and he only lived a half block up the street, yet here she was, waving to him as if he was going to Japan. 90

At the door of his car, it seemed stupid to him to drive the measly half block home. His old coach, Bob Behn, used to say never to ride where you could walk. Cars were the death of legs. Ace left the ignition keys in his pocket and ran along the pavement with Bonnie laughing and bouncing at his chest. He slammed the door of his landlady's house 95 open and shut, pounded up the two flights of stairs, and was panting so hard when he reached the door of his apartment that it took him a couple of seconds to fit the key into the lock.

The run must have tuned Bonnie up. As soon as he lowered her into the crib, she began to shout and wave her arms. He didn't want to play 100 with her. He tossed some blocks and a rattle into the crib and walked into the bathroom, where he turned on the hot water and began to comb his hair. Holding the comb under the faucet before every stroke, he combed his hair forward. It was so long, one strand curled under his nose and touched his lips. He whipped the whole mass back with a 105 single pull. He tucked in the tufts around his ears, and ran the comb straight back on both sides of his head. With his fingers he felt for the little ridge at the back where the two sides met. It was there, as it should have been. Finally, he mussed the hair in front enough for one little lock to droop over his forehead, like Alan Ladd. It made the temple seem 110 lower than it was. Every day, his hair-line looked higher. He had observed all around him how blond men went bald first. He remembered reading somewhere, though, that baldness shows virility.

What does this elaborate hair-combing tell us about Ace?

On his way to the kitchen he flipped the left-hand knob of the television. Bonnie was always quieter with the set on. Ace didn't see 115 how she could understand much of it, but it seemed to mean something to her. He found a can of beer in the refrigerator behind some brownish lettuce and those hot dogs Evey never got around to cooking. She'd be home any time. The clock said 5:12. She'd pop her lid.

Ace didn't see what he could do but try and reason with her. 'Evey,' 120 he'd say, 'you ought to thank God I got out of it. It had no future to it at all.' He hoped she wouldn't get too mad, because when she was mad he wondered if he should have married her, and doubting that made him feel crowded. It was bad enough, his mother always crowding him. He punched the two triangles in the top of the beer can, the little triangle first, and then the big one, the one he drank from. He hoped Evey wouldn't say anything that couldn't be forgotten. What women didn't seem to realize was that there were things you knew but shouldn't say. 125

He felt sorry he had called the kid in the car a wop.

Ace balanced the beer on a corner where two rails of the crib met and looked under the chairs for the morning paper. He had trouble finding his name, because it was at the bottom of a column on an inside sports page, in a small article about the county basketball statistics: 130

> 'Dusty' Tremwick, Grosvenor Park's sure-fingered center, copped the individual scoring honors with a season's grand (and we do mean grand) total of 376 points. This is within eighteen points of the all-time record of 394 racked up in the 1949-1950 season by Olinger High's Fred Anderson. 135

Ace angrily sailed the paper into an armchair. Now it was Fred Anderson; it used to be Ace. He hated being called Fred, especially in print, but then the sportswriters were all office boys anyway, Behn used to say. 140

'Do not just ask for shoe polish,' a man on television said, 'but ask for *Emu Shoe Gloss*, the *only* polish that absolutely *guarantees* to make your shoes look shinier than new.' Ace turned the sound off, so that the man moved his mouth like a fish blowing bubbles. Right away, Bonnie howled, so Ace turned it up loud enough to drown her out and went into the kitchen, without knowing what he wanted there. He wasn't hungry; his stomach was tight. It used to be like that when he walked to the gymnasium alone in the dark before a game and could see the people from town, kids and parents, crowding in at the lighted doors. But once he was inside, the locker room would be bright and hot, and the other guys would be there, laughing it up and towel-slapping, and the tight feeling would leave. Now there were whole days when it didn't leave. 145 150

Try to put into your own words how Ace feels. Why did he feel this way when he was a basketball player? Why does he feel like this now?

A key scratched at the door lock. Ace decided to stay in the kitchen. Let *her* find *him*. Her heels clicked on the floor for a step or two; then the television set went off. Bonnie began to cry. 'Shut up, honey,' Evey said. There was a silence. 155

'I'm home,' Ace called.

'No kidding. I thought Bonnie got the beer by herself.'

Ace laughed. She was in a sarcastic mood, thinking she was Lauren Bacall. That was all right, just so she kept funny. Still smiling, Ace eased into the living room and got hit with, 'What are *you* smirking about? Another question: What's the idea running up the street with Bonnie like she was a football?' 160

'You saw that?' 165

'Your mother told me.'
'You saw her?'
'Of course I saw her. I dropped by to pick up Bonnie. What the hell do you think? – I read her tiny mind?'
'Take it easy,' Ace said, wondering if Mom had told her about 170 Friedman.
'Take it easy? Don't coach *me*. Another question: Why's the car out in front of her place? You give the car to her?'
'Look, I parked it there to pick up Bonnie, and I thought I'd leave it there.' 175
'Why?'
'Whaddeya mean, why? I just did. I just thought I'd walk. It's not that far, you know.'
'No, I don't know. If you'd been on your feet all day a block would look like one hell of a long way.' 180
'Okay. I'm sorry.'

What kind of mood is Evey in?

She hung up her coat and stepped out of her shoes and walked around the room picking up things. She stuck the newspaper in the wastebasket.
Ace said, 'My name was in the paper today.' 185
'They spell it right?' She shoved the paper deep into the basket with her foot. There was no doubt; she knew about Friedman.
'They called me Fred.'
'Isn't that your name? What *is* your name anyway? Hero J. Great?'
There wasn't any answer, so Ace didn't try any. He sat down on the 190 sofa, lighted a cigarette, and waited.
Evey picked up Bonnie. 'Poor thing stinks. What does your mother do, scrub out the toilet with her?'
'Can't you take it easy? I know you're tired.'
'You should. I'm always tired.' 195
Evey and Bonnie went into the bathroom; when they came out, Bonnie was clean and Evey was calm. Evey sat down in an easy chair beside Ace and rested her stocking feet on his knees. 'Hit me,' she said, twiddling her fingers for the cigarette.
The baby crawled up to her chair and tried to stand, to see what he 200 gave her. Leaning over close to Bonnie's nose, Evey grinned, smoke leaking through her teeth, and said, 'Only for grownups, honey.'
'Eve,' Ace began, 'there was no future in that job. Working all Saturday, and then Friday nights on top of it.'
'I know. Your mother told *me* all that, too. All I want from you is what 205 happened.'
She was going to take it like a sport, then. He tried to remember how it *did* happen. 'It wasn't my fault,' he said. 'Friedman told me to back this '51 Chevvy into the line that faces Church Street. He just bought it from an old guy this morning who said it only had thirteen thousand on 210 it. So in I jump and start her up. There was a knock in the engine like a machine gun. I almost told Friedman he'd bought a squirrel, but you know I cut that smart stuff out ever since Palotta laid me off.'
'You told me that story. What happens in this one?'

'Look, Eve. I *am* telling ya. Do you want me to go out to a movie or something?'

'Suit yourself.'

'So I jump in the Chevvy and snap it back in line, and there was a kind of scrape and thump. I get out and look and Friedman's running over, his arms going like *this*' – Ace whirled his own arms and laughed – 'and here was the whole back fender of a '49 Merc mashed in. Just looked like somebody took a planer and shaved off the bulge, you know, there at the back.' He tried to show her with his hands. 'The Chevvy, though, didn't have a dent. It even gained some paint. But *Friedman,* to *hear* him – Boy, they can rave when their pocket-book's hit. He said' – Ace laughed again – 'never mind.'

Evey said, 'You're proud of yourself.'

'No, listen. I'm not happy about it. But there wasn't a thing I could *do*. It wasn't my driving at all. I looked over on the other side, and there was just two or three inches between the Chevvy and a Buick. *Nobody* could have gotten into that hole. Even if it had hair on it.' He thought this was pretty good.

She didn't. 'You could have looked.'

'There just wasn't the *space*. Friedman said stick it in; I stuck it in.'

'But you could have looked and moved the others cars to make more room.'

'I guess that would have been the smart thing.'

'I guess, too. Now what?'

'What do you mean?'

'I mean now what? Are you going to give up? Go back to the Army? Your mother? Be a basketball pro? What?'

'You know I'm not tall enough. Anybody under six-six they don't want.'

'Is that so? Six-six? Well, please listen to this, Mr. Six-Foot-Five-and-a-Half: I'm fed up. I'm ready as Christ to let you run.' She stabbed her cigarette into an ashtray on the arm of the chair so hard the ashtray jumped to the floor. Evey flushed and shut up.

How do you think this scene will end?

What Ace hated most in their arguments was these silences after Evey had said something so ugly she wanted to take it back. 'Better ask the priest first,' he murmured.

She sat right up. 'If there's one thing I don't want to hear about from you it's priests. You let the priests to me. You don't know a damn thing about it. Not a damn thing.'

'Hey, look at Bonnie,' he said, trying to make a fresh start with his tone.

Evey didn't hear him. 'If you think,' she went on, 'if for one rotten moment you think, Mr. Fred, that the be-all and end-all of my life is you and your hot-shot stunts –'

'Look, Mother,' Ace pleaded, pointing at Bonnie. The baby had picked up the ashtray and put it on her head for a hat and was waiting for praise.

Evey glanced down sharply at the child. 'Cute,' she said. 'Cute as her daddy.'

The ashtray slid from Bonnie's head and she patted where it had been and looked around puzzled. 265

'Yeah, but watch,' Ace said. 'Watch her hands. They're really terrific hands.'

'You're nuts,' Evey said.

'No, honest. Bonnie's great. She's a natural. Get the rattle for her. Never mind, I'll get it.' In two steps, Ace was at Bonnie's crib, picking 270 the rattle out of the mess of blocks and plastic rings and beanbags. He extended the rattle toward his daughter, shaking it delicately. Made wary by this burst of attention, Bonnie reached with both hands; like two separate animals they approached from opposite sides and touched the smooth rattle simultaneously. A smile bubbled up on her face. Ace 275 tugged weakly. She held on, and then tugged back. 'She's a natural,' Ace said, 'and it won't do her any good because she's a girl. Baby, we got to have a boy.'

'I'm not your baby,' Evey said, closing her eyes.

Saying 'Baby' over and over again, Ace backed up to the radio and, 280 without turning around, switched on the volume knob. In the moment before the tubes warmed up, Evey had time to say, 'Wise up, Freddy. What shall we do?'

The radio came in on something slow: dinner music. Ace picked Bonnie up and set her in the crib. 'Shall we dance?' he asked his wife, 285 bowing.

'I want to talk.'

'Baby. It's the cocktail hour.'

'This is getting us no place,' she said, rising from her chair, though.

'Fred Junior. I can see him now,' he said, seeing nothing. 290

'We will have no Juniors.'

In her crib, Bonnie whimpered at the sight of her mother being seized. Ace fitted his hand into the natural place on Evey's back and she shuffled stiffly into his lead. When, with a sudden injection of saxophones, the tempo quickened, he spun her out carefully, keeping 295 the beat with his shoulders. Her hair brushed his lips as she minced in, then swung away, to the end of his arm; he could feel her toes dig into the carpet. He flipped his own hair back from his eyes. The music ate through his skin and mixed with the nerves and small veins; he seemed to be great again, and all the other kids were around them, in a ring, 300 clapping time.

See Glossary section at the back of the book for vocabulary.

First reaction

2 Does the end of the story offer any hope for Ace and Evey's future, or does it show only a moment of temporary relief?

3 How do you feel at the end of the story?

Close reading

Judging characters

4 What are the important things in Ace's life? Look at the list of ideas below and

a) decide where to put each of them on the scale showing their relative importance or unimportance to Ace (you can decide to put two or more in the same place on the scale if you want).

b) refer to at least one sentence or passage from the story to support your opinion.

Scale

0 1 2 3 4 5 6 7 8 9 10

unimportant — important

Write a number 1–10 referring to the scale	Reference from the story to support your opinion
__ work	lines ________
__ his wife	lines ________
__ his child	lines ________
__ sport	lines ________
__ the past	lines ________
__ the future	lines ________
__ his mother	lines ________
__ his appearance	lines ________
__ a trouble-free life	lines ________
__ pleasure	lines ________

c) Discuss your answers to **a)** and **b)** with another student.

Here are some ways that you can talk about your decisions:

I think . . . is (much) more/(much) less important to Ace than . . .
I think . . . is (much) more/less important to Ace than . . .
I think . . . and . . . are equally (un)important to him.

5 Look at these dictionary definitions of *ace* and *hole*

ace/eɪs/*n* **1** playing card with a large single spot, usu having the highest or lowest value in card games: *the ace of spades.* **2** *(infml)* person who is an expert at some activity: [attrib] *an ace pilot, footballer, marksman, etc.* **3** (in tennis) stroke, esp a service, that is too good for the opponent to return. **4** (idm) (**have**) **an ace up one's sleeve;** *US* (**have**) **an ace in the hole** *(infml)* (have) sth effective kept secretly in reserve. **play one's ace** use one's best resource. **within an ace of sth/doing sth** very near to (doing) sth: *He was within an ace of death/being killed.*

hole/həʊl/ *n* **1** [C] (**a**) sunken or hollow place in a solid mass or surface cavity: *a hole in a tooth* ○ *roads full of holes.* (**b**) opening through sth; gap: *The prisoner escaped through a hole in the wall* ○ *I've worn holes in my socks.* ○ *My socks are in holes/full of holes,* ie worn so much that holes have formed. ○ *a hole in the heart,* ie a defect at birth in the membrane of the heart. **2** [C] (**a**) animal's burrow: *a mouse hole* ○ *a fox's hole.* (**b**) (usu *sing) (fig infml)* small, dark or unpleasant room, flat, district, etc: *Why do you want to live here – it's a dreadful hole!* **3** [sing] (*sl*) awkward or difficult situation: *be in (a bit of) a hole.* **4** [C] *(sport)* (**a**) hollow or cavity into which a ball, etc must be hit in various games: an *eighteen-hole golf-course.* (**b**) (in golf) section of a golf course between a tee and a hole; point scored by a player who reaches the hole with the fewest strokes: *win the first hole.* **5** (idm) **have an ace in the hole** ⇨ ACE. **a hole in the wall** very small dingy shop, café, etc, esp in a row of ɔf buildings. **make a hole in sth** *(infml)* use a large amount of (one's money, supplies, etc): *The hospital bills made a big hole in his savings.* **money burns a hole in sb's pocket** ⇨ MONEY. **pick holes in sth** ⇨ PICK.

(Oxford Advanced Learner's Dictionary)

a) Why does the protagonist prefer 'Ace' to Fred (lines 138-41)?

b) What do you think the real meaning of the title of the story is? Is Updike using the idiom *ace in the hole* ironically?

6 'It was funny how, though the whole point was to get the ball up into the air, kids grabbed it by the sides and squeezed. Kids just didn't think.' (lines 73-5)

Do you think this is ironic? Is there any contrast in the story between Ace's physical ability and his intellectual and emotional development?

7 Do you agree or disagree with these statements? Why?

	Agree	*Disagree*
a) Ace's attempt to patch up the quarrel with Evey is motivated more by wanting an easy life at home than by love.		
b) Ace lives in the past: in fact, he has not matured at all since his youth.		
c) Ace's wife is obviously more intelligent than her husband.		
d) Bonnie is the important element in the relationship between Ace and Evey.		
e) Ace is a fool, but an interesting fool.		

Language practice

Criticising and complaining
wish + past tense; *wish* + *would* + base form of verb

8 Evey uses this particular quarrel to bring out a long list of criticisms of Ace – criticisms which she is surely not making for the first time.

Match the ideas in the right hand column with the statements in the left hand column. (You will need to use three of the ideas from the right hand column twice.)

What Evey says in this quarrel

a) 'What's the idea running up the street with Bonnie like she was a football?' (lines 163-4)
b) 'Why's the car out in front of her place? You give the car to her?' (lines 172-3)
c) 'If you'd been on your feet all day a block would look like one hell of a long way.' (lines 179-80)
d) 'What *is* your name anyway? Hero J. Great?' (line 189)
e) ([Ace] 'I know you're tired.') 'You should. I'm always tired.' (lines 194-5)
f) 'I know. Your mother told

Evey's general criticisms of Ace

i) You don't try to understand anything about my religion. Don't criticise my beliefs.
ii) You never tell me what really happens – you always make up stories about what happens.
iii) You're irresponsible and careless. You never stop to think of the consequences of your actions
iv) You're too involved in your past glories and not involved enough in the present.
v) You never think of *me*. You think more of your mother than you do of me.

me all that, too. All I want from you is what happened. . . . You told me that story. What happens in this one?' (lines 205-6, 214)

g) 'You're proud of yourself . . . you could have looked and moved the other cars to make more room.' (lines 227, 235-6)

h) 'I mean now what? Are you going to give up? Go back to the Army? Your mother? Be a basketball pro? What?' (lines 240-1)

i) 'If there's one thing I don't want to hear about from you it's priests. You let the priests to me. You don't know a damn thing about it. Not a damn thing.' (lines 251-3)

j) 'Wise up, Freddy. What shall we do? . . . This is getting us no place.' (lines 282-3, 289)

vi) You never think about the future. You don't try to plan ahead. You aren't realistic.

vii) You don't appreciate how hard I work. You never think of *me*.

a) ____________ **b)** ____________ **c)** ____________

d) ____________ **e)** ____________ **f)** ____________

g) ____________ **h)** ____________ **i)** ____________

j) ____________

Do you think that most quarrels are like this – a particular incident which provokes a more or less permanent list of criticisms? Which comment hurts Ace most, do you think? Which comment would hurt you most?

9 Evey uses a very rich variety of language when she criticises Ace (although Ace certainly does not appreciate this!). There are, for example, a lot of direct, accusing questions as well as rhetorical questions. She also makes great use of irony.

There are other ways of criticising and complaining available in English. Look at these possibilities.

a) *wish* + person you are criticising + past tense (often used with *be* and *have*); for example:

He's such a dreamer! I *wish* he *wasn't* such a dreamer!

You have too many mad ideas!	I *wish* you *didn't have* so many mad ideas!

b) *wish* + person you are criticising + *would* + base form of the verb; for example:

You always arrive late!	I *wish* you *would* arrive earlier/on time! I *wish* you *wouldn't* always arrive late.
You never tell me anything!	I *wish* you *would* tell me things! I *wish* you *wouldn't* be so secretive!

c) the present progressive form with the adverb *always* (only with action verbs, not with state verbs) ; for example:

You criticise me all the time!	You'*re always criticising* me!

10 Look again at the right hand column in question 8. Re-state Evey's criticisms using an appropriate structure with *wish*. Where can you use the present progressive form?

Example

i) You don't try to understand anything about my religion. Don't criticise my beliefs.	I *wish* you *would* try to understand my religion. I *wish* you *wouldn't* criticise my beliefs. You'*re always criticising* my religious beliefs!

11 a) Choose a social context – husband and wife, parent and son/daughter, two friends, two colleagues at work – and write down five criticisms that one person might make of the other using an appropriate structure with *wish* or the present progressive form.

b) Re-state the criticisms using any language except *wish* or the present progressive (or pass your criticisms to another student to re-state).

12 Are there any complaints or criticisms that you have of your partner or a member of your family? Does he/she have any complaints or criticisms of you?

I (sometimes) *wish* my husband/girlfriend etc. *would/wouldn't*...
was/wasn't. . .
My husband/girlfriend etc. (sometimes) *wishes* I *had/didn't have*

Vocabulary

Generic and specific words

13

Generic words	fruit	furniture	go
Specific words	apple banana grape orange etc.	bed sofa table chair desk etc.	walk run jog race stroll etc.

a) What generic word do the specific words *enormous, huge, gigantic* relate to?
b) What generic word do the specific words *Pontiac, Mercedes, Chevrolet* relate to?
c) What generic word do the specific words *rattle, block, beanbag* relate to?
d) Give some specific words for the generic word *sport.*

14 Updike shows Ace's character partly through the way he behaves. Ace, the ace sportsman, never performs actions in an ordinary way: he does them with style. Observe Ace at the beginning of the story, making himself feel better by doing such an ordinary thing as lighting a cigarette as if he were performing a brilliant move at basketball.

'. . . from the pack pinched between the car roof and the sun shield he *plucked* (**1**) a cigarette, *hung* (**2**) it on his lower lip, *snapped* (**3**) a match across the rusty place on the dash, held the flame in the instinctive spot near the tip of his nose, *dragged* (**4**), and blew out the match, all in time to the music. He *rolled down* (**5**) the window and *snapped* (**6**) the match so it *spun* (**7**) end-over-end into the gutter. 'Two points,' he said, and *cocked* (**8**) the cigarette towards the roof of the car, *sucked* (**9**) powerfully, and *exhaled* (**10**) two plumes through his nostrils. He was beginning to feel like himself, Ace Anderson . . .' (lines 9–17)

Updike of course uses adverbs and adjectives to great effect, but the use of specific instead of generic words contributes to the effect of this passage. One could describe this process of lighting a cigarette with generic words, but then it could be anybody in the car, not Ace Anderson. Experiment with this effect by matching the descriptive, specific verbs in the passage above with the more generic, less descriptive verbs given below.

breathe in throw put breathe out take out move (the position of) go pull open

1)____ **2)**____ **3)**____ **4)**____ **5)**____ **6)**____ **7)**____ **8)**____ **9)**____ **10)**____

15 Look at Ace performing some other action with his usual sportsmanlike panache. In each case, give a more general description of what he does. Do this without looking back at the vocabulary notes to the story.

a) Ace *flicked on* the radio. (line 2) turned on.

b) Ace *dug out* so hard . . . (line 32) ________

c) He *slammed* the door of his landlady's house open and shut, *pounded* up the two flights of stairs . . . (lines 95-6) ________

d) He *tossed* some blocks and a rattle into the crib . . . (line 101) ________

e) He *whipped* the whole mass back . . . (line 105) ________

f) . . . he *flipped* the left-hand knob of the television. (line 114) ________

g) He *punched* the two triangles in the top of the beer can, . . . (lines 124-5) ________

h) Ace angrily *sailed* the paper into an armchair. (line 138) ________

i) . . . Ace *eased* into the living room . . . (line 161-2) ________

j) So I *jump in* the Chevvy and *snap* it back in line, (line 218) ________ ________

Extension

16 Discussion

Is it important for the effect of *Ace in the Hole* that Ace is a retired sportsman? Would the story have the same effect if he were an ex-financier, or a retired scientist, or an ageing actor?

17 What might a marriage guidance counsellor say to Ace and Evey?

18 Composition

Imagine that Evey decides that she has had enough, and leaves Ace. Write the note that she would leave him. (about 150-200 words)

Beyond the text

A Natural Sportsman

19 a) Look at this extract from *The Natural*, by Bernard Malamud (1952). (His short story *The First Seven Years* is in Chapter 4).

Roy Hobbs was potentially a great baseball player, a 'natural', but just at the beginning of his career he was shot by a mad girl fan. Years later, when he is 34, he starts his career all over again. In this extract, we see Roy in the early days with his new team. He feels alienated from them, partly because he is so much older, and is subject to alternating feelings of power and weakness.

The words in the box – specific rather than generic words – are the words Malamud uses. Put them back into the extract.

muttered	weakening	joined	gazing	watch
crawl away	draining	squinting	squirted	hammered

Roy sat around, and though it said on his chest he was one of the team, he sat among them alone; at the train window, (**1**) ____________ at the moving trees, in front of his locker, absorbed in an untied shoe lace, in the dugout, (**2**) ____________ at the great glare of the game. He travelled in their company and dressed where they did but he (**3**) ____________them in nothing, except may be batting practice. . . . Almost always he (**4**) ____________ the swift, often murderous throws (the practice pitchers dumped their bag of tricks on him) deep into the stands, as the players watched and (**5**) ____________ at the swift flight of the balls, then forgot him when the game started. But there were days when the waiting got him. He could feel the strength (**6**) ____________ from his bones, (**7**) ____________ him so he could hardly lift Wonderboy. He was unwilling to move then, for fear he would fall over on his puss and have to (**8**) ____________ on all fours. Nobody noticed he did not bat when he felt this except Pop; and Bump, seeing how white his face was, (**9**) ____________ contemptuous tobacco juice in the dust. Then when Roy's strength ebbed back, he would once again go into the batters' cage and do all sorts of marvellous things that made them (**10**) ____________ in wonder.

Vocabulary

1 chest: *large suitcase*
4 dugout: *place from where baseball players watch the game*
9 dumped their bag of tricks: *did all their best throws*
9 stands: *part of the ground where the spectators stand*
14 Wonderboy: *the name Roy has given to his personal bat*
15 on his puss (US slang): *on his face*
16 Pop: *the trainer*
17 Bump: *another player in the team*

20 Is there any feeling Roy experiences which is similar to the feelings experienced by Ace? Is it only sportsmen who feel like this?

Author

John Updike was born in 1932, brought up in Pennsylvania and studied at Harvard University. During a year's study at Oxford University in England, he sold a poem to *The New Yorker* magazine. On returning to New York he worked for this magazine before becoming a full-time writer. Updike has written poetry and criticism, but is best known for his novels and short stories. These, generally set in small towns, often deal with the difficulties of human relationships. His best known novels are *Rabbit, Run* (1960), *Rabbit Redux* (1971) and *Rabbit is Rich* (1981), about the life of ex-basketball star Harry Angstrom and his difficult marriage (*Ace in the Hole*, 1959, may have been the origin of this trilogy), and *Couples* (1968), about the marital problems of young, middle-class couples. More of his excellent short stories can be found in *Pigeon Feathers and Other Stories* (1962), *Museums and Women* (1972), and *Problems and Other Stories* (1979).

Glossary

The Open Window

1 self-possessed: *confident*
5 without unduly discounting: *without giving the impression he wasn't interested in*
12 a living soul: *anybody*
13 mope: *to feel sad and low when one is alone*
23 pursued: *continued*
34 French window: *large window that opens like a door*
40 snipe: *a kind of bird*
41 engulfed: *swallowed up*
41 treacherous: *dangerous*
41 bog: *wet ground that sucks a person under so that he drowns*
45 falteringly: *hesitatingly*
47 spaniel: *a kind of dog*
51 bound: *to jump*
53 creepy: *strange, uncanny*
55 shudder: *a shiver, a trembling because of fear*
56 bustled into: *came quickly into*
63 marshes: *wet ground, similar to bogs (see line 41)*
65 rattled on cheerfully: *talked happily*
68 ghastly: *horrible, awful*
75 laboured under the tolerably widespread delusion that . . .: *thought, wrongly, like many others that . . .*
76 chance acquaintances: *people one happens to meet accidentally*
92 was additionally burdened with: *also carried*
96 gravel-drive: *private road to the house*
97 dimly noted stages in his headlong retreat: *he ran away and hardly noticed these things*
102 bolted out: *ran away*
108 pariah dogs: *wild dogs*
109 snarl: *to show the teeth in a menacing way*
110 foaming: *with saliva coming out of the mouth*

Under the Banyan Tree

1 nestling away: *lying almost hidden*
3 sink: *become depressed*
3 tank: *container for water supply*
5 malaria, typhoid: *kinds of disease*
6 sprawled, twisted, wriggled, strangled: *all verbs which show how the streets have developed without any planning*
12 enchantment/enchanter: *magician's spell/ magician*
15 cut off: *isolated, far from the nearest town*
16 reckoning: *counting*
26 Shakti: *Hindu goddess*
26 sanctum: *the holiest part of the temple*
27 for aught it mattered: *not that it mattered much*
30 dhoties (Indian word) : *loose covering worn around the waist and upper legs*
31 banyan: *Indian species of fig tree (Ficus Indica)*
37 squatted: *sat*
39 sourly: *unpleasantly*
45 a score: *twenty (here: about twenty)*
46 threshold: *entrance*
50 niche: *a space, a hollow*
57 ablaze: *shining brightly (like a fire)*
57 ash and vermilion: *dust left from burnt wood, and a red dye or paint*
60 jerk: *to move quickly*
68 durbar hall (Indian word) : *king's hall or room in a palace*
68 vassal: *subject, inferior to*
78 babble: *noisy talking*
82 jostled each other: *crowded together*
89 prostrate: *to lie on the ground on one's stomach (a position of worship and prayer)*
95 drab: *dull, uninteresting*
101 mumble: *to speak indistinctly, so that the words can't be heard*
102 stumble: *to make mistakes*
108 utter: *complete*
109 he flared up: *he said angrily*
131 dry up: *to run out of ideas, to be unable to continue*
132 stammer: *to speak hesitatingly*
138 dwindle: *to grow less*
142 harrowed: *tormented, extremely worried*
160 dotard: *a fool*
161 jasmine: *a flower with a sweet scent*
169 gesture: *movement of the hands*
173 consummate: *complete*

A Dill Pickle

11 muff: *a roll made of wool or fur to warm the hands in cold weather*
23 loathe: *to hate*
30 settle: *to agree*
30 just a hint: *just a little*
34 exasperate: *to frustrate*
42 grave: *serious*
45 haunting: *coming back again and again*
50 geranium, marigold, verbena: *names of flowers*
55 scene: *embarrassing situation*
57 wasps: *flying insects that sting*
59 snigger: *to laugh at someone secretly*
63 linger: *to remain*
67 lap: *the part between the waist and the knees when someone is sitting*
71 dodge: *to move quickly*
85 she hovered over them: *she hesitated while looking at them*
103 slumber: *to sleep*
104 stir: *to wake up and move yourself*
104 bound: *to leap, jump*
116 grimace: *an expression of pain or annoyance*
122 bond: *a feeling of being united*
135 a dill pickle: *a small cucumber preserved in vinegar with dill, an aromatic herb added to give extra flavour*
140 velvet: *a soft, luxurious material*
144 parasol: *a sun-shade*
144 crochet hook: *hooked needle like a knitting needle*
147 parrot: *an exotic bird*
152 boundless: *without limit*
155 mournful: *sad*
160 mockery: (*n*) *making fun of someone, laughing at someone*
160 fancy: *imagination*
165 yard: *space behind a house*
170 seven and sixpence: *seven shillings and six pence; old British currency before decimalisation. (37½p), a lot of money in 1920.*
182 snapped to: *closed quickly*
186 drummed: *made a rhythmic noise with his fingers*
192 veil: *piece of net material attached to a hat which can be drawn down over the face*
210 purr: *to make a soft, contented noise. Cats make this noise.*
225 scraped his chair: *moved his chair so quickly it made a noise*
227 self-engrossed: *occupied exclusively with oneself*
229 hearty: *very loud and cheerful*

First Confession

Note: Roman Catholics believe in the idea of *confession*. If one has committed a sin one goes to *confess* to a priest. Sincere *contrition* (sorrow for sin) must be expressed. After hearing the confession, the priest gives *absolution* (pardon) on condition that one does *penance* (an act of atonement) : this usually involves saying prayers, for example the prayer beginning 'Hail Mary . . .'. *Communion* is the ceremony where Catholics take wine and bread, which symbolise the blood and body of Christ. The first communion must be preceded by confession so that all sins are absolved.

6 the boots had her crippled: *boots hurt her feet so much she couldn't walk in them*
7 porter: *strong beer*
9 relish: *enjoyment*
11 fastidious: *insisting on delicacy and good manners*
12 suck up to (colloquial): *to try to please by being excessively polite*
16 steering up: *walking unsteadily up*
17 mortified: *very embarrassed*
22 to let on (Irish dialect): *pretend to be*
23 saw through her: *realised what she was really like*
24 to side with: *to take the side of, to agree with*
24 I lashed out at her: *I tried to cut her*
28 gave me a flaking (Irish dialect): *beat me*
30 heart-scalded (Irish dialect): *very upset*
31 to crown: *to complete*
33 the one age with: *the same age as*
34 bonnet: *hat*
36 the other place: *heaven*
39 half-crown: *old British coin (12½p)*
55 husky: *hoarse, with a voice that comes from a dry throat*
60 was after making (Irish dialect): *had made*
61 cock: *male chicken*
61 crow/crew/crowed: *make the noise made by a cock, particularly at dawn*
68-71 the four questions here come from the Ten Commandments in the Bible
68 take the name of the Lord in vain: *to blaspheme*
71 covet (archaic/Biblical): *to envy, to want something that belongs to someone else*
89 shin: *front part of leg between foot and knee*
90 Lemme go (colloquial): *let me go*
106 chapel yard: *open space in front of the church*
108 yelp: *shout*
108 hurl: *to throw*

110 dirty little caffler (Irish dialect): *very naughty boy*
116 wedged me in: *sat on my other side*
119 muttering aspirations: *praying*
126 as if butter wouldn't melt in her mouth: *sounding very innocent*
129 aisle: *corridor between seats in a church*
134 of itself: *by itself*
135 pitch-dark: *completely dark*
137 He had all the odds: *everything was in his favour*
142 He had me spotted all right: *he certainly knew who I was*
143 one height with: *the same height as*
146 on the high side: *rather high*
149 nothing you could get a grip on: *nothing to hold*
149 moulding: *ornamental strip of wood surrounding a window or opening*
160 it struck me: *it seemed to me*
163 to rattle off: *to say very quickly*
163 the least shade more: *just a little more*
168 hit the door an unmerciful wallop: *hit the door very hard*
171 biretta: *hat worn by priests*
178 gave me a clip across: *smacked, hit*
180 maimed: *wounded, injured*
182 you little vixen: *you naughty girl*
184 cocking an outraged eye: *looking outraged, offended*
186 giving me a hand up: *helping me to stand up*
194 get rid of you: *finish with you*
199 I couldn't even be bothered retorting: *I didn't feel I needed to reply*
205 cackle: *silly meaningless talk*
207 barring: *except for*
209 steered: *guided*
211 grille: *the window with bars between the two parts of the confessional box*
217 shaken: *shocked*
227 snuff: *powdered tobacco sniffed through the nose*
234 chop up: *cut into small pieces*
234 barrow: *kind of container on wheels used in the garden*
236 Begor (Irish dialect): *By God*
242 go for: *to attack*
245 have the nerve: *to dare*
245 hanging: *form of capital punishment: the condemned man is executed by being hung from a rope passed around his neck*
255 in the religious line: *involved in religion*
258 screech: *a noise made when vehicles brake*
259 soar: *to leap, jump (my heart soared: I suddenly felt happy)*
262 railing: *fence*
262 a very sour puss (colloquial): *a very disappointed face*
263 mad (colloquial) : *very*
279 with a baffled air: *looking puzzled, confused*
283 bullseye: *a kind of sweet*

The First Seven Years

Note: Feld (like Sobel) is a Polish Jew who has emigrated to the USA. His English is not standard American English; it is influenced by Yiddish, the language spoken by Jews in Eastern and Central Europe. You will find some examples of his deviation from standard American English at lines 71, 204, 242, 289, 299-301...

2 reverie: *daydream*
3 pound: *to hammer, to beat*
4 last: *iron object in the shape of a foot on which shoemakers put shoes when working*
6 near-sighted haze: *the snow makes everything indistinct*
7 blur: *indistinct mass*
10 trudge: *to walk with great effort*
12 dire: *severe, extreme*
16 diligence: *hard work*
16 peddler: *someone who sells things of small value on the street*
23 grieve: *to cause grief, to upset*
26 battered: *in bad condition because of constant use*
28 tremble: *to shake quickly because of excitement*
28 discern: *to recognise*
36 harp on: *to insist*
38 meddle: *to interfere*
38 let by: *to ignore*
42 connivance: *plot, scheme*
48 come to grips with: *to recognise*
65 alert: *attentive*
65 grotesque: *very unpleasant to look at*
67 slushy: *wet with snow*
68 draped over: *hanging over*
68 soggy: *very wet*
78 hawk: *large bird which catches other birds and small animals for food*
86 flighty: *always changing one's mind*
100 clanging: *loud noise made when metal is hit*
108 temperamental: *with quickly changing moods*
109 carry: *to manage*

111 exert oneself: *work hard*
112 sacrifice . . . block: *sell to the person who offered the most money*
113 pittance: *very small amount of money*
114 unscrupulous: *immoral*
115 refugee: *someone who leaves his country for political reasons*
117 stocky: *short but strong and muscular*
118 prone to tears: *tending to cry*
121 apt: *he learnt quickly*
122 landsman: *someone from the same country*
127 till: *drawer where shopkeeper puts the money taken from customers*
131 profuse: *abundant*
131 queer: *strange*
132 rooming house: *a house with rooms to let cheaply*
133 peer at: *to look closely at*
133 twitched: *moved nervously*
146 stew: *to stay alone and reconsider things*
147 taxed: *over-used*
148 nagging: *insistent, repeated*
150 fancied slight: *imagined insult*
152 in a huff: *angrily, in a bad mood*
157 burly: *large and strong*
166 rasp: *cough*
176 aftermath: *what happens after*
179 his type: *men like him*
181 snap: *to answer angrily*
188 hunched: *with shoulders bent over*
218 deft: *skilful*
221 accountancy: *keeping records of the financial business of people and companies, and analysing them*
223 bookkeeper: *a bookkeeper simply records money transactions*
231 probe: *to ask more questions*
236 volunteer: *to give information without being asked*
237 non-committal: *giving no real information or personal attitude*
242 What . . . word?: *What does this word mean?*
259 Adam's apple: *prominent part of the larynx, in the front of the throat*
263 crumpled: *old and worn*
263 newly-minted: *new (a mint is a coin factory)*
268 mild: *not serious*
269 rose in wrath against: *reacted angrily to*
273 toil up: *to walk up with great trouble*
276 cot: *small bed*
277 haphazardly: *in no particular order*
286 stubby: *short and thick*
287 pallid: *white*
288 bolt: *to run away*
295 to be at a loss: *not to know*
300 vehemently: *passionately*
303 hoarse: *rough (as when suffering from a cold)*
304 croak: *to speak roughly, hoarsely*
307 stingy: *mean, insufficient*
310 blurt: *to say something suddenly*
312 seethe: *to boil*
330 sobs: *noise made when you cry*
330 fists clenched: *hands closed tightly*
335 by the skin of his teeth: *scarcely, only just*
335 Hitler's incinerators: *ovens where the Nazis burned the bodies of Jews and other people*
338 ease his heart: *express his feelings*
357 pounding: *hammering*

The Nightingale and the Rose

Note: Wilde's language is sometimes deliberately poetic and archaic (dating from a previous period; the abbreviation *arch.* is used in the vocabulary notes). This does not reflect the normal prose style of the time when Wilde was writing; it is intended to create a magical, beautiful, 'fairy tale' atmosphere. You will notice that after line 167 the style loses its poetic flavour – you will want to consider why. See question 5, Close Reading. Examples of a deliberately poetic style are the frequent inversions (eg lines 9-10 Night after night have I sung of him) and the repetitions (eg lines 61-2 My roses are yellow . . . as yellow as . . . and yellower than . . .)

3 holm-oak: *an evergreen oak tree (Quercus ilex)*
3 nightingale: *kind of bird (Daulias luscinia) with beautiful song; it sings by night*
8 for want of (arch.): *because I don't have*
11 Hyacinth-blossom: *the flower on the dark purple hyacinth plant (Hyacinthus orientalis)*
13 ivory: *material that elephants' tusks are made of*
13 set her seal: *marked*
15 ball: *splendid party with dancing*
19 clasp: *to hold*
20 have no heed of (arch.): *pay no attention to*
25 pomegranates: *an exotic fruit (Punica Granatum)*
25 set forth: *set out, displayed for sale*
31 throng (arch.): *to crowd*
34 wept: (present tense weep) *cried*
35 lizard: *a small reptile with legs*
37 butterfly: *flying insect with beautiful wings*
37 flutter: *to fly in a light, irregular way*
39 daisy: *common white flower with yellow centre (Bellis perennis)*

43 cynic: *anti-romantic person who doubts human values*
46 soar: *to fly quickly high into the air*
47 grove: *a small group of trees*
50 lit upon (arch.): *landed on*
50 spray: *flowering branch*
53 foam: *the white froth made by waves as they break*
55 sun-dial: *stone 'clock' in a garden that tells the time as the shadows from the sun move across it*
62 mermaiden: *mythical sea creature; beautiful woman from head to waist, with a fish's tail*
62 amber: *rich yellow-orange coloured substance used for making jewellery*
63 daffodil: *yellow Spring flower (Narcissus pseudo-Narcissus)*
63 mower: *person who cuts grass*
64 scythe: *tool for cutting grass*
70 dove: *white bird (often used as a symbol of peace)*
71 coral: *a hard, red substance, found in the sea; formed from the skeletons of small animals, it looks like a plant*
72 nipped my buds: *stopped my flowers growing*
83 pierce: *penetrate, go into*
87 chariot (arch.): *carriage pulled by horses*
88-9 hawthorn, bluebells, heather: *plants and flowers (Crataegus, Hyacinthoides non-scripta, Erica)*
100 mighty (arch.): *powerful, strong*
103 frankincense: *an exotic perfume*
114 she has form: *her music is technically perfect*
121 pallet-bed: *cheap, simple bed*
127 ebbed away from her: *left her*
130 petals: *the part of the flower that surrounds its centre*
131 feet of the morning: *early dawn*
141 flush: *act of turning red (eg one's face flushes with embarrassment)*
144 crimson: *to turn deep red; also, the colour red*
152 tomb (arch.): *grave, place where the dead are buried*
154 girdle (arch.): *belt; here, it means the petals surrounding the centre*
157 film: *a layer of water, making the vision unclear*
160 linger: *to stay*
174 wind: *to twist round and round*
175 reel: *cylindrical object for keeping cotton or silk on*
178 next: *next to*
181 go with: *to match, to make a good combination of colours*
182 Chamberlain (arch.): *person who managed the royal household*
189 buckle: *part of a shoe*
194 unpractical (the normal form is impractical): *of no use, unrealistic*

Outside the Cabinet-Maker's

1 Sixteenth: *Sixteenth Street, a street in New York*
1 dingy-looking: *with a dirty, rather sad appearance*
9-10 Dites .. bois (French): *Say it doesn't have to have strong walls . . . Or good wood.*
13 Et .. ça (French): *And it must have a good height . . . the one the Murphys had was like that.*
15 Cabinet-Maker: *furniture maker, carpenter*
17 red brick: *the buildings were made of red bricks; this means there was nothing unusual about them*
17 darkies: *black people* (darkies *would now be an offensive term)*
23 mask: *to hide*
24 faint stir: *a little movement*
25 shutter: *a wooden 'door' outside the window*
27 Fairy: *magical spirit*
42 yawn: *to breathe in deeply with the mouth wide open (when one is tired or bored)*
46 story: *floor of a building*
50 christening: *baptism, ceremony in church when a baby is given his Christian name (first name)*
51 President Coolidge: *President of the USA from 1923 to 1929*
51 collar-box: *box for keeping shirt collars*
59 Aroused: *excited*
62 disguised: *with changed appearance*
62 Mombi in 'The Land of Oz': *a character in an American children's story*
73 linger: *to wait*
75 crisp: *fresh*
78 sidewalk (American English): *pavement*
80 charm: *a magic spell*
92 Witch: *bad woman with magic powers in fairy stories*
101 unmartial: *not looking like a soldier*
106 trance: *day-dream*
108 cake: *block*
112 a yellow darky's overcoat: *a coat normally worn by black people doing manual work (at the time of this story)*
113 upholstery: *material to put on furniture such as chairs and sofas*
117-18 luster and texture: *brightness and consistency*

120 limp: *walk unevenly*
122 abstractedly: *while thinking of something else*
124 ragged: *torn and in bad condition*
124 blinds: *coverings for windows*
129-32 Il dit .. Vingt-cinq (French): *He said he made the doll's house for the Du Ponts. He's going to do it. How much? Twenty-five (dollars).*
142 too summarily disposed of: *killed too quickly*
148 odd doings: *strange events*

Lamb to the Slaughter

1 drawn: *closed*
2 sideboard: *piece of furniture; drawers and cupboards with a surface on top for putting things on*
4 Thermos bucket: *container for keeping things cold*
11 with child: *pregnant*
11 translucent: *clear*
12 placid: *calm*
15 gravel: *small pieces of stone used to make a path or drive*
26 blissful: *extremely happy*
33 strides: *paces*
40 drain: *to drink from a glass or cup until it is empty*
48 amber: *orange*
52 sip: *to drink slowly*
53 swirls: *curling patterns*
63 stuff: *things*
65 nod: *an up-and-down movement of the head, meaning 'yes'*
67 crackers: *biscuits*
81 bewildered: *confused and worried*
93 dazed: *shocked and confused*
98 fuss: *trouble, scandal*
99 it occurred to her: *she thought*
101 went about her business: *continued normally*
122 club: *thick, heavy stick used as a weapon*
125 sway: *to move slowly from side to side, or backwards and forwards*
128 blink: *to open and close one's eyes quickly*
133 penalty: *the punishment for a crime*
141 shove: *to push*
149 rehearse: *to practise (it normally refers to practising a scene in a play)*
159 catch: *to surprise*
180 tasty: *with a good taste, delicious*
183 frantic: *desperate*
191 hum: *to sing softly with the lips closed, without saying the words of the song*
196 longing: *desire*
196 well up: *to rise up*
197 to cry one's heart out: *to cry passionately*
205 sob: *to speak while crying*
206 Be right over: *we'll come immediately*
209 precinct: *area of a town or city where a policeman works*
216 congealed: *hard, no longer wet*
222 mutter: *to speak softly*
228 slip out: *to go out*
239 corpse: *dead body*
239 stretcher: *a kind of bed used for transporting dead or wounded people*
243 put someone up: *let someone sleep in your house*
256 administered: *given*
256 blunt: *not sharp*
259 premises: *the house*
264 spanner: *a metal tool, used for turning nuts and bolts*
272 chink: *a small gap*
273 mantel: *shelf above the fireplace*
274 a trifle exasperated: *a little frustrated*
283 a drop: *a small drink*
284 a nip: *a small drink*
288 on: *switched on*
305 Wouldn't dream of it: *I would never consider the idea*
306 beg: *to ask insistently*
314 sloppy: *wet*
320 the hell of a (slang): *very*
321 doc (slang): *doctor*
321 skull: *the bones of the head*
322 sledge-hammer: *very heavy hammer used for breaking bricks and stone*
327 belch: *to make a noise from your mouth as a result of eating too much*
329 under one's nose: *(metaphorically) very near; Dahl also plays on the literal meaning of this phrase*
330 giggle: *to laugh softly, but uncontrollably*

Ace in the Hole

3 tubes: *parts of the radio*
4 She'll pop her lid: *She'll get really angry*
5 irk: *to irritate*
6 static: *interference on the radio*
8 Blueberry Hill: *famous pop song of the 1950s*
10-14 Ace lights a cigarette and throws away the match. *For verbs used in lines 9-16, see Vocabulary section*
14 gutter: *channel between pavement and road*
18 jerk: *to move suddenly*
21 bust: *break*

21 blared: *shouted*
22 '52 Pontiac: *Pontiac car manufactured in 1952*
25 Shove it (mildly offensive): *Go away*
31 wop: *slang term of abuse, referring to Italians, Greeks and Spaniards*
32 dig out: *start moving*
33 lurch: *to move abruptly*
36 stall: *to cause a car's engine to stop*
42 fire: *to dismiss an employee from his/her job*
52 had the brains to get out of it: *were intelligent enough to leave*
62 dribbling a basketball: *running while bouncing a basketball*
63 backboard: *piece of wood behind basketball net*
72 let . . . go by: *to ignore*
73 funny: *strange*
74 squeeze: *to press from both sides*
77 so what?: *what's important about that?*
78 I guess (US English): *I suppose (British English)*
80 dopey: *sleepy*
80 she fussed: *she wasn't quiet*
85 blink: *to close and open one's eyes quickly*
85 nicely: *skilfully*
87 walk: *path*
89 jiggle: *to vibrate*
91 measly: *insignificantly small*
92 coach: *sports trainer*
96 pound: *run or stride heavily*
96 pant: *to breathe quickly after running*
99 tuned Bonnie up: *made her feel awake and wanting attention*
100 crib: *baby's bed with tall sides*
101 rattle: *baby's toy which makes a noise when one shakes it*
103 faucet (US English): *tap (British English)*
104 strand: *collection of hairs together*
106 tufts: *protruding short hairs*
108 ridge: *prominent line*
109 muss: *to put slightly into disorder*
109 lock: *curl*
110 droop: *to hang down*
110 Alan Ladd: *handsome film star of the 1940's and 1950's*
110 temple: *side of the forehead*
115 set: *television*
118 hot dogs: *kind of sausage*
118 get around to doing: *to find the time to do*
122 mad (US English slang): *angry*
134 copped: *won*
135 grand: *final (in 'grand total') and great*
137 racked up: *scored*
146 howl: *to cry loudly*
146 to drown her out: *to make more noise than her*
151 locker room: *changing room*
156 honey: *darling, dear*
159 No kidding (US English slang): *Really?*
160 Lauren Bacall: *film actress who starred in a series of 1940s thrillers with Humphrey Bogart; these films were distinguished by the witty, sarcastic conversation between Bacall and Bogart*
161 just so she kept funny: *as long as she stayed sarcastic*
162 smirk: *to smile in a satisfied way*
168 dropped by: *went there*
170 Take it easy: *Calm down*
177 Whaddeya mean? *What do you mean?*
186 shove: *to push*
192 stink: *to have a bad smell*
193 scrub out: *clean*
198 Hit me (slang): *Give me a cigarette*
198 twiddle: *to move impatiently*
202 leak: *to escape*
204 on top of it: *as well*
207 take it like a sport: *be reasonable about it*
209 '51 Chevvy: *Chevrolet car manufactured in 1951*
210 thirteen thousand on it: *it had done 13,000 miles*
212 bought a squirrel: *made a bad buy*
213 I cut that smart stuff out: *I stopped making those funny comments*
213 laid me off: *fired me, dismissed me*
215 ya: *you*
217 Suit yourself: *Do what you want*
218 back in line: *in the line of cars again*
219 scrape and thump: *the noises made by the cars coming into contact*
220 whirl: *to move in circles*
221 '49 Merc: *Mercedes car manufactured in 1949*
221 mashed in: *dented*
222 planer: *carpenter's tool for smoothing wooden surfaces*
224 dent: *a depression in the metal*
225 rave: *to shout angrily and uncontrollably*
225 pocket-book: *wallet*
230-1 Nobody . . . hair on it: *Ace makes an obscene joke; he is referring to a woman's sexual parts*
234 stick it in: *put it in the space*
241 pro: *professional player*
242 six-six: *6 feet 6 inches (just over 2 metres) tall*
245 let you run: *leave you*
245 stab: *push violently*
247 Evey flushed: *Evey's face went red*
252 let: *to leave*
257 the be-all and end-all: *the most important thing*

258 hot-shot (US English): *brilliant, very talented*
258 stunts: *tricks*
259 plead: *to beg, ask desperately*
262 cute (US English): *charming*
268 nuts (US English slang): *mad*
269 a natural: *(she has) natural talent*
273 wary: *cautious*
276 tug: *to pull*
280 backed up to: *walked backwards to*
282 Wise up (US English): *Be sensible*
289 no place (US English): *nowhere*
292 whimper: *to cry softly*
294 she shuffled stiffly into his lead: *she moved reluctantly to follow his movements in the dance*
295-297 he spun her out . . . end of his arm: *they are dancing 'rock and roll'; she alternately moves away from him and close to him as they hold hands*

Key

1 Short Stories and tall tales

1 i-h; ii-b; iii-e; iv-c; v-g; vi-a; vii-f; viii-d.

2 i-d; ii-c; iii-ab; iv-h; v-e; vi-g; vii-f. Sentences, iii, iv, vi make positive comments. Sentences i, ii, v, vii make negative comments.

5 WHO? **a)** Mr. (Framton) Nuttel, **b)** the niece (Vera), **c)** the aunt (Mrs. Sappleton).
WHERE? **b)**
b) WHEN? It takes place at the time the author wrote the story, but this is not important for the effect of the story.
WHAT situation? Framton Nuttel is recovering from a nervous breakdown and has gone to the country. His sister has given him the addresses of some people in the country he may want to visit.
WHAT happens next? Mrs. Sappleton's niece starts to make up the story of her aunt's tragedy.
WHAT happens as a result? When Mrs. Sappleton appears she says she is expecting her husband and brothers so Framton finds the situation horrible and tries to change the subject.
WHAT happens finally? Mrs. Sappleton sees her husband and brothers returning and Framton thinks they are ghosts so he runs away.

6 **a)** To make sure that Framton knows nothing and so will have no reason to doubt her story.
b) Lines 86-9; she pretends to be horrified.

7 WHO? Mrs. Sappleton, her husband and her brothers.
WHERE? The Sappleton's house and surrounding country.
WHEN? Three years previously.
WHAT situation? Mrs. Sappleton's husband and brothers went out shooting.
WHAT happens next? They were drowned in a bog. Their bodies were never found.
WHAT happens as a result of that? Mrs. Sappleton still hopes they will return.
WHAT happens finally? [the story might finish *they came back as ghosts* – this is what Framton, who is drawn into Vera's story, thinks]

10 WHO? Nambi is a very old man, illiterate but a brilliant inventor of stories, who seems to be a sort of unofficial priest to the Goddess Shakti. The villagers are poor and apparently apathetic about their economic and social conditions.

WHERE? The village Somal, in the forest of Mempi (somewhere in India we assume from the names and our knowledge of the writer), which is backward, underdeveloped and isolated.

WHEN? The story doesn't seem to be set in a historical period; it seems to be set at the same time as the author wrote the story (lines 2-3 seem to set the story in modern times). But the village is so backward and isolated that its lifestyle belongs to previous rather than modern times.

WHAT situation? The villagers are enchanted by Nambi's story-telling, addicted to it, we might almost say, and willingly feed and clothe him.

WHAT happens next? **i)** See the paragraph at lines 96-106, **ii)** in particular the sentences at lines 98-9. 'He paused. He could not get beyond it.'

WHAT happens as a result? Nambi realises he is old and suspects his powers might be failing, but tries to continue with the story. He finds, however, that he can't.

WHAT happens finally? Nambi invites everyone to the temple and says that his gift of story-telling is finished. From then on he never speaks again.

11 Nambi's stories had exotic settings (lines 61-72), and a wide variety of characters, who were much higher in social status than the audience (lines 80-2); they were exciting and emotional (lines 84-7). He was a good performer and told his stories at the most suitable time (lines 83-4). Spreading the story over several nights – several instalments – probably created suspense. [Do you see any similarities with some television soap operas?]

12 Suspense (lines 101-146): What is Nambi going to do? and (lines 147-57) What is his story going to be like? Surprise (lines 163-4): He doesn't tell a story.

13 [suggested response] It is natural that age brings a reduction in one's powers and talents. One should accept this with philosophical resignation instead of desperately trying to continue as before, which will only bring undignified failure.

14 The verb in the past perfect tense (*had* + past participle) refers to an action or state that happened before the verb in the past continuous or simple.

15 1 **e)** 2 **d)** 3 **b)** 4 **c)** 5 **a)** 6 **f)**

16 1 had started 2 invited 3 decided 4 arrived 5 had spent 6 went 7 had taken 8 had happened 9 had already eaten 10 wondered 11 certainly didn't want 12 had taken 13 carved 14 had done 15 was 16 went 17 had completely forgiven 18 opened 19 had happened 20 was 21 had happened 22 had obviously died 23 had eaten 24 called 25 told 26 agreed 27 said 28 went 29 saw 30 had not noticed

The story would certainly be different if the narrative sequence was the same as the chronological sequence. If the reader was told that the neighbour had run over the cat before the description of the dinner there would be no surprise for the reader. To take another example, consider how different a murder story would be if the murder and the name of the murderer were described fully at the beginning of the story!

17 Bond woke up. His head was aching. He tried to move but he found he couldn't. Someone had tied him to the bed! Then he remembered what had happened the night before. He had said goodnight to Tatania and had gone up to his hotel room. He had switched on the light and seen Olga sitting on his bed. Then someone had hit him hard on the head and he had fallen unconscious to the floor. He wondered where Olga was now.

20 **a)** Myths, legends, parables and folk-tales were originally told orally, but are now found in written collections. Jokes and anecdotes are usually told orally.

c) There are many connections that you can make. Here are some obvious ones. There are very close similarities between the following, indeed some of the genre names are almost synonymous: detective and crime stories/whodunnits; ghost and horror stories/spine chillers; thrillers/adventure stories; romantic and love stories/tear-jerkers; myths and legends/folk-tales; jokes/anecdotes and tall stories. In addition, you might consider that many popular genres have the same kind of main characters. For example, although spy stories, Westerns, science fiction stories and legends have different settings, the main characters are often heroes and villains, good characters and bad characters.

25 [suggested response] It seems to say that the things one most wants in life end in disappointment and disillusion; a rather tragic vision of life.

2 Love in vain

2 a) It seems that the woman has been more moved by this meeting. The questions in Close reading invite you to consider this response in more detail.

b) She probably leaves because what the man says in lines 225-32 shows her that he has no intention of starting another relationship with her. It is also possible that she suspects he is being deliberately cruel to her.

3 [suggested response]
'Yes, I should like that': How romantic, how wonderful! How I would love to experience those things.
'Yes, I know perfectly what you mean': This is what I really want from life.
'Yes, I'm afraid I must': I can't bear to be here any longer.
'Not a bit': I feel very hurt.
'Yes, just the same. I am as alone as ever': Is there a chance? Could we get together again?

4 [open response] How you answer depends on how you judge the man. Is he being *deliberately* insensitive to the woman, or has he simply changed from the way he was into a less sensitive person? Or do we even admire him for the way he has recovered from this love affair? When at the end of the story he asks not to be charged for the cream, the reader probably reconsiders his character less favourably: a few pennies are more important to him than the effect of his meeting with Vera.

5 [open response] The woman suspects, perhaps, he is deliberately taking some kind of revenge on her because she left him. Or has he just changed? The reader, like the woman, cannot be sure, but finds the meeting painful.

6 a) **ii)** He didn't use to have much money (and perhaps he wanted to make money). **iii)** The man says that he used to be deeply in love with her; he used to feel that she was the only person he could talk to.

b) **i)** She used to be rather a solitary person. **ii)** She used to have desires for a romantic and exotic life. **iii)** She used to feel he was a similar person to herself.

c) **i)** He thinks he used to be immature. **ii)** He used to think she was a lonely but exceptional person. **iii)** He thinks they both used to be selfish and used to consider only themselves.

7 a) **i)** He still peels oranges in a particular way.
ii) He still interrupts people.

iii) She still has a beautiful voice.
iv) He still doesn't know the names of flowers.
v) He isn't poor any more./He is no longer poor.
vi) He doesn't remember the name of his dog any more./ He no longer remembers the name of his dog.

b) [open response] You might have considered:
i) It seems that she recognizes she still loves him, or at least could love him again (lines 215-18). She is still alone and hasn't found anyone else (line 222). He says he is still alone (line 223), but what he says at lines 226-8 suggests he no longer feels he needs or wants her. We know, from lines 169-83, that she remembers more of their love affair, while he seems to have forgotten details. This implies he still means something to her.
ii) The reader is not told, as the man is not told, whether she has sold her piano because she has lost money, or because romance has passed out of her life. We only know that it is something unpleasant for her.

11 The man makes the comparison between himself and a carpet, and between the unpleasant aspects of life and sharp mud and stones. This suggests that he offered himself as something soft and protective for her, something that would hide and protect her from the rough, ugly aspects of life. He then extends the metaphor, comparing himself to a magic carpet, suggesting that he would have been able to realise all her desires to travel and see exotic places.

12 [These suggested interpretations are deliberately very full; if you have mentioned some of the following ideas you have probably understood the metaphors.]
a) This is a metaphor in two parts. In the first part the 'boundless understanding between them', which is a mutual emotional and intellectual understanding, is compared to a physical embrace: 'their souls . . . put their arms around each other'. This suggests the completeness of their understanding. It then continues with the comparison between their souls and two mournful lovers content to be drowned in the same sea. This gives the idea of a mutual love that is immense but in some way impossible, so that it can only escape from the world rather than live in it. It also suggests a complex mixture of happiness and sadness.
b) In this metaphor the woman is compared to the glove that the man is holding. This suggests something about the relationship between them. She is something soft that he can caress and also manipulate as he wants. It gives the idea that he can pick her up or put her down; he is in control. It also

suggests something sensual – she would enjoy being caressed and stroked by him.

15 [These are the actual words used. Your suggestions may also be correct – check with your teacher or a native speaker]

1) wear **2)** memory **3)** your **4)** sing **5)** haunt **6)** on **7)** love **8)** hold **9)** danced **10)** life

3 Childhood memories

4 a) the adult Jackie **b)** the boy Jackie **c)** the adult Jackie **d)** the boy Jackie **e)** the boy Jackie

5 a) lines 219-26; 228; 233; 244-5; 248;
b) gloomily (193); He seemed a bit shaken (217); and I could see he was impressed (226); he asked with great interest (233); he said rather cryptically (243); he said solemnly (248); he said with great satisfaction (250).

6 Lines 201-6; 223; 227; 229-32; 246-7 (in an adult this would be a morbid interest); 259-61.

7 This is probably, but not necessarily, a comment on religious bigotry. It is not simply a childish thought.

9 a) He said that mine were the crimes of a lifetime and that he didn't know if he would get rid of me at all today/that day. He told me I'd better wait until he was/had finished with those old ones. He said I could see by the looks of them that they hadn't much to tell.
b) He said that that would be a shocking thing to do and asked me what had put that into my head.
c) He agreed with me that that was a bad case.
d) He asked me if I realised that I was a terrible child.
e) He remarked that someone would go for her with a bread-knife one day. He told me that I had to have great courage. He confided that there were a lot of people he would like to do the same to but he had never had the nerve. He pointed out that hanging was an awful death.
f) He assured me that it was a horrible death. He went on to say that lots of the fellows that he had seen had killed their grandmothers too, but they all said that it was never/had never been worth it.

10 a) She asked me what he had given me.
b) She wanted to know whether I had told him about Gran and all.

- **c)** She asked if I had told him that I'd gone for her with the bread-knife.
- **d)** She asked again if he had only given me three Hail Marys.
- **e)** She wanted to know if it was the priest that had given them to me.
- **f)** She complained that some people had all the luck, and that it was no advantage trying to be good. (She said that) She might just as well be a sinner like me.

11 The sudden introduction of direct speech at lines 27-8 and 45-7 has a vivid, dramatic effect, giving the reader a sense of being present at the scene.

12 **a)** pretended **b)** pretended **c)** real **d)** pretended **e)** could be pretended or real (but the connotation of 'cocking' suggests an intended rather than automatic action, leading the reader to suspect that this is more pretended than real) **f)** real **g)** real

13 **b)** regretfully **c)** triumphantly

14 with a smile, smiling; excited, in an excited voice/tone; with a look of horror; with a puzzled look; as if he had never heard the word before; in a depressed tone (Note: *in a depressed voice* is not a normal collocation); with a feeling of disgust; as if she had just seen a ghost; laughing, or with a laugh.

18 **a)** Passage **1** **b)** Passage **2**

19 [suggested response; you could make other comments]

- **a)** Passage **1:** Yes **2:** No
- **b)** In both passages we can detect certain attitudes: in passage **1** affection, wonder, admiration; and in passage **2** a sense of the strangeness of the world.
- **c)** There is no comment, helping to give the impression that the narrator cannot interpret what is happening. A narrator who could interpret the events (for example, a first person narrator looking back in the past) might possibly add 'I lisped' or 'I tried to repeat the song', after line 11.
- **d)** In passage **1** the vocabulary is not simple (eg pocket nutmeg grater) because an adult is speaking with a full command of an adult's vocabulary and a full understanding of the situation he is remembering, while in passage **2** the vocabulary is very simple: a monocle (one lens worn as glasses are now) and a beard are described in paraphrase to give the idea that the child doesn't understand them and doesn't know the names for them (lines 4-5).
- **e)** In passage **1** the sentences are long and complex, in passage **2** they are short. The narrator of passage **1,** the adult David, has a complete vision of the scene he is describing, and the long sentences reflect this completeness. The narrator of passage **2** imitates a child's understanding of the world: he

doesn't see or understand a complete situation, but only one thing at a time. The short sentences reflect this.

4 Romance

3 a) [in the order of the narrative] his physical description, containing negative words like 'grotesquely' and 'beak-like' (lines 65-6) (see the Language practice section later in this chapter for detailed work on Malamud's use of physical description) ; the way he looks in line 78, so unemotional and presented with the image of a predator; his questions in lines 79-86 – is he being merely sensible, or do we judge him as being cold?; the way he immediately starts talking of money matters (lines 93-5) – do we suspect he is asking for a special price because he is going to go out with Miriam?

b) 'Max's Adam's apple went up once when he saw them, and his eyes had little lights in them. 'How much?' he asked, without directly looking at the shoemaker.' (lines 259-61) He is only interested in his shoes and the price he will have to pay. He is pleased and surprised at the fine appearance of his shoes, but perhaps worried that he will have to pay more as he is not going out with Miriam. He does not want to talk about Miriam. His physical reactions suggest a combination of nervousness, excitement, embarrassment and meanness.

4 a) lines 2-4; 55-6; 101-2; 336-8; 356-7. He works for Feld so that he can be near Miriam. He works so hard perhaps to get rid of his frustration at not being able to court Miriam openly, perhaps to lose himself and sublimate his love for Miriam in work.

b) It seems clear that Malamud intends us to sympathise with Sobel. One might point to his honesty, his diligence, his passion for reading, his passion for Miriam, the fact that he has suffered in the past, and even the poignant contrast between his physical appearance and the depth of his feelings.

5 a) lines 97-9; 112-114; 136-9; 168-170; 199-200; 293; 311-12.

b) We doubtless judge him much more kindly than we judge Max because his work and his wanting to make money are caused by his desire for a better life for Miriam (lines 345-6), and by genuine need (lines 111-14). He has also voluntarily paid more money – if not much more – to Sobel (lines 135-6).

c) [A personal response] There has been some kind of business deal between the two men: the cheap price for the shoe repair job in return for Max going out with Miriam. This mixture of materialism with 'romance' reflects badly on both men. But the adjectives used for the money seem to also refer to the two men, so that while Max seems 'crumpled' by this exchange (morally 'dirty') Feld comes out of it morally 'cleaner'.

d) **i)** The two contradictory expressions are 'with a stronger stride' (line 354) and 'heavy-hearted' (line 355). **ii)** He feels stronger because he and Sobel have faced the truth together; and he feels heavy-hearted because his ambitions for Miriam have been defeated.

6 **a)** Just let him once . . . for sure be interested. (lines 43-4)
b) Or suppose Miriam . . . for his meddling? (lines 36-8)
c) . . . let her marry . . . better life. (line 49)
d) But he had not dared . . . he face him again? (lines 35-6)
e) Maybe he would . . . go to college. (lines 47-8)

Would is used to show what would definitely happen if a condition was fulfilled. *Might* is used to show what could possibly happen if a condition was fulfilled.

7 **1)** asked **2)** would not suffer **3)** would/might not feel **4)** did **5)** would/might not realise **6)** dismissed **7)** would be **8)** would definitely earn **9)** might even open **10)** would have **11)** was/were not **12)** might be **13)** had **14)** might steal **15)** would get **16)** auctioned **17)** would not be able **18)** would have to **19)** would be **20)** did

8 Open response to the questions. The questions are formed like this:

a) If Feld ordered Miriam not to talk to Sobel how would she react? How would Sobel react?
b) If Feld had second thoughts and dismissed Sobel what would Sobel do? What would Miriam do?
c) How would Feld feel if Sobel and Miriam ran away together?
d) What would Sobel do if Miriam rejected him?
e) If Sobel and Miriam got married would they be happy? What kind of life would they have? Would they still be happy if they never had enough money?

f) Would Miriam have a 'better' life if she married a man with career prospects?

9 Sobel paradoxically seems both young and old. Max is tall, thin and compared to a hawk, but his clothes are loose, slushy, soggy, battered, droopy, etc.; there is a contradiction between something large and menacing and something feeble, uncared for and unimpressive.

10 Open response, but you might have thought of the following. (Note that we do not *know* that the men are like this, but we *suspect* it from the description.)

Max: sinister, cruel, awkward, untrustworthy, unpleasant, mean, insecure, insensitive [sad, vulnerable are possible too]

Sobel: sad, pathetic, vulnerable, reliable, awkward, spiritual, honest, sensitive, [insecure, clever are possible too]

Neither: humorous, stupid

11 b) Their clothes. Max: lines 67-8; 188; Sobel: 285. Their clothes seem to be rather obvious symbols of their spirituality: Sobel's clean despite his poverty, Max's ill-fitting and adding to his sense of social inadequacy.

15 **1)** lips **2)** hair **3)** distinctive **4)** smell **5)** anyone **6)** eyes **7)** black **8)** kisses **9)** breath **10)** description

16 Almost certainly **b)**

17 a) Can you give me a precise description?; Were there any noticeable Peculiarities?; Any particular Colour?; It has been established; are you implying that Violence was used?; I regret that we know of No one answering to that description.

b) It would be unlikely for a policeman to say: Could you give me, . . . a metaphor?

c) It is rather a cryptic ending, but it seems that, as soon as passion and poetry enter into the description (lines 19-21), the policeman quickly avoids any suggestion of sexual feeling and dismisses it as being of no further use. He even stands up, in order to end the interview as swiftly as possible. Perhaps the poet suggests that a subjective, emotional description of a loved one and an objective description are fundamentally incompatible.

5 Fairy tales

3 **1)** h **2)** b **3)** l **4)** d **5)** k **6)** a **7)** f **8)** e **9)** i **10)** c **11)** j **12)** g.

4 The nightingale visits three rose trees; the white, the yellow and the red (lines 49-74). You might also have noticed the nightingale's song has three distinct phases (lines 128-34; 138-40; 149-52) which make the red rose, before her 'last burst' (lines 159-64), which signals her death.

5 The romantic attitude to love represented by the nightingale is replaced by the pragmatic attitude of the student and the girl.

6 **1)** who **2)** but **3)** Unfortunately **4)** While **5)** because (or, as) **6)** Then (or, So) **7)** and **8)** This time **9)** which **10)** because of (or, after) **11)** By now **12)** Reluctantly (or, Eventually) **13)** After **14)** Despite **15)** Eventually (or, Soon) **16)** as **17)** The next day **18)** however **19)** so **20)** soon (or, eventually)

7 ungrateful, idealistic, unselfish, superficial, materialistic, vain, sympathetic, romantic, generous, unimaginative

9 -ity; practicality, sensitivity, sentimentality, sincerity, insincerity, egocentricity
-ion: compassion, education, passion
-ness: tenderness, kindness, shallowness, rudeness, unhappiness
-ism: cynicism, sentimentalism, realism

13 Open response, but the following statements are probably the most likely: **a)** i; **b)** ii; **c)** ii; **d)** i or iii; **e)** i **f)** iii **g)** iii

14 a) We can see the man improvising at lines 61-80; he makes the small boy an ogre, his drawing magic signs and his dancing a magic dance. Lines 81-5; the two men. Lines 93-6; the shutter opening and closing. Lines 100-1; Mr Miller. Lines 108-10; the man carrying the cake of ice.

b) Reality behaves conveniently when the woman's response is made inaudible by the wind (lines 73-5). She might have said something completely incongruous. The boy's words are also inaudible.

16 Open response, but the questions are formed like this:
What would the father have said if . . . a fire engine had come down the street/ if the woman had come out of the flat/ if a police patrol had walked past/ if a group of children had started playing outside the flat/ if the small boy had said. . .?

17 Usual combinations would be:
hesitate + uncertainly, abstractedly;
scream + impatiently, loudly;
mutter + sleepily, inaudibly, complainingly, softly, sarcastically;
sneer + mockingly, sarcastically; *exclaim* + impatiently, loudly;
whisper + inaudibly, romantically, patiently, softly, lovingly;
explain + politely, patiently; *yawn* + sleepily, loudly;
shout + impatiently, loudly, menacingly;
grumble +impatiently, complainingly; *stutter* + uncertainly;

sigh + impatiently, complainingly, softly, sarcastically, lovingly; *call* + impatiently, loudly, softly, menacingly.

But other combinations are possible in certain contexts. For example, an actor on stage would whisper loudly, as would someone who deliberately wanted to be overheard.

24 These are Thurber's words. Your answers might also be correct. Check with your teacher or a native speaker.
1) for **2)** carrying **3)** Finally **4)** and **5)** asked **6)** her **7)** told **8)** wood **9)** door **10)** that **11)** on **12)** than **13)** saw **14)** wolf **15)** does **16)** grandmother **17)** So **18)** out **19)** as (or, so)

In fairy stories a 'suspension of belief' is expected from the reader. This means that the most incredible things happen, which the reader would never believe in real life, yet he/she accepts them in the context of a fairy story. In the traditional version of *Red Riding Hood,* the little girl thinks that the wolf in bed is her grandmother. Thurber emphasises how ridiculous this would be in real life, and *his* heroine recognises the wolf immediately.

Also, heroines in fairy stories are always innocent and ingenuous. Not Thurber's heroine, who draws a pistol and shoots the wolf. (Interestingly, Thurber himself makes use of the reader's 'suspension of belief'. If you think about it, it is *most* unlikely that a little girl would have a pistol in her basket!)

6 Whodunnit?

3 a) His drinking (lines 40-1; 48-9; 52-3; 58-8) What he says and the way he speaks to her (lines 20 [no 'darling']; 39 [no 'darling']; 47 [a brusque imperative]; 61 [no 'darling' or 'thanks']; 56; 65-6 he doesn't answer; 68 [no 'darling' or 'thanks']; 73 [a brusque imperative]; 77, 79.
b) The way he treats his wife when he comes home (although the stress of the situation might make this natural). After he has told her he is going to leave her the mention of fuss being bad for his job is a selfish concern. One might also consider that leaving his wife during her pregnancy is immoral.

4 Answers that are justifiable from the story are:
a) ii **b)** iii, iv **c)** i **d)** i, iii **e)** ii, iv **f)** i, iii **g)** i, ii **h)** i **i)** ii, iii **j)** Because she doesn't want to run the risk of being executed before her child is born.

5 c) seems most likely.

7 a) to create **b)** so that she can keep **c)** so that her grief will appear **d)** so as not to endanger **e)** so that Sam won't notice

f) so that they can examine **g)** to check **h)** so that the evidence will be destroyed **i)** so that Mary won't/can't hear **j)** so as not to cause

9 **a)** 1.d, 2.g, 3.h, 4.b, 5.k, 6.c, 7.l, 8.j, 9.f, 10.a, 11.e, 12.i.

b)
1) They used a stolen car for the getaway so that the police wouldn't be able to/couldn't connect the car to them.
2) She asked her best friend to say that they had been to the cinema together so that she would have an alibi.
3) He carefully wiped all the surfaces he had touched so that he wouldn't leave any fingerprints.
4) They always telephoned from a public telephone box so that the police wouldn't be able to/couldn't trace the phone calls.
5) They had a driver waiting outside in a fast car so that they would be able to/could make a quick getaway.
6) She fitted a silencer onto the pistol so that the shot wouldn't/couldn't be heard.
7) They sent a message from the girl recorded on a cassette so that her parents would know she was still alive.
8) He didn't take anything that was exceptionally valuable so that he wouldn't have any difficulty selling it.
9) They put women's tights over their faces so that no-one would be able to/could recognise them.
10) He left the back door open so that he would be able to/could run away quickly if necessary.
11) She took the dead man's wallet so that the police would think the motive was robbery.
12) They asked for the money to be paid in used banknotes of small denomination so that the police wouldn't be able to/couldn't trace the money.

c)
i) murder: 2, 3, 5, 6, 9, 10, 11
ii) bank robbery: 1, 2, 5, 9, 12
iii) burglary: 1, 2, 3, 5, 8, 9, 10
iv) kidnapping: 1, 4, 5, 7, 9, 12

10 Open response, but some suggestions are:
a) so that nobody would recognise him/to change his appearance
b) so that they could hear what he said/so that they would hear his conversations
c) to make them go to sleep/so that they (the dogs) would go to sleep
d) She arranged a perfect alibi/She pretended to be very upset
e) He was reading a newspaper/ He behaved as a tourist

f) They put everything back in the right place/They destroyed all the evidence

11 **c)** horror, horrify, horrified, horrifying. **d)** shock, shock, shocked, shocking **e)** surprise, surprise, surprised, surprising **f)** exasperation, exasperate, exasperated, exasperating **g)** satisfaction, satisfy, satisfied, satisfying **h)** worry, worry, worried, worrying **i)** fascination, fascinate, fascinated, fascinating **j)** pleasure, please, pleased, pleasing **k)** annoyance, annoy, annoyed, annoying **l)** amusement, amuse, amused, amusing **m)** outrage, outrage, outraged, outrageous **n)** fright, frighten, frightened, frightening **o)** charm, charm, charmed, charming **p)** embarrassment, embarrass, embarrassed, embarrassing **q)** frustration, frustrate, frustrated, frustrating **r)** delight, delight, delighted, delightful **s)** disappointment, disappoint, disappointed, disappointing **t)** disgust, disgust, disgusted, disgusting

12 **a)** e, g, i, j, l, o, r
b) a, b, c, d, e, f, h, k, m, n, p, q, s, t
c) and **d)** [Open response]

16 **1)** observation **2)** deduction **3)** impulse **4)** simplicity **5)** explanation **6)** avoid **7)** know **8)** rest **9)** send **10)** remains

7 The Sporting Life

4 [Open response] Generally speaking, you will probably have decided that sport and pleasure, together with nostalgia for the golden days of the past (also reflected in his concern with looking young), are more important for Ace than the everyday responsibilities of work, family and the future. These responsibilities make him feel 'crowded' (as he expresses his feeling in line 123). Some of the references from the story (although you might have quoted others) which lead to this conclusion are:

Work: lines 48-50; 120-2; 218-43. His wife: lines 60-1; 120-4; 126-7. His child: lines 99-103; 115; 146-7; 255-6; 260. Sport: lines 14-15; 33-5; 62-4; 72-5; 92-8. The past: 138-41; 299-301. The future: lines 277-8; 290. His mother: lines 84; 88-90; 124. His appearance: lines 103-13. A trouble-free life: lines 47-50; 148-53; 160-1; 207. Pleasure: lines 7-20; 298-301.

5 **a)** 'Ace has the connotations given at **2** in the definition of 'ace' from *The Oxford Advanced Learner's Dictionary*, while 'Fred' (abbreviation of 'Frederick') was an extremely common name for men of Ace's generation. He wants to sound special.

b) Probably the use is ironic. Most importantly, Ace is *in a hole,* that is, a difficult, even desperate situation (**3** of definition of 'hole'). Secondly, although he tries to play an *ace in the hole* – his suggestion that he and Evey have another baby – we suspect strongly that this will come to nothing.

6 Surely there is. Ace constantly thinks of, and indulges in, the subtle movements of the body. His thinking is less advanced.

8 **a)** iii **b)** v **c)** vii **d)** iv **e)** vii **f)** ii **g)** iii **h)** vi **i)** i **j)** vi

10 **ii)** I wish you would tell me what really happens. I wish you wouldn't always make up stories about what happens. You're always making up stories about what happens.
iii) I wish you weren't so irresponsible and careless. I wish you would stop to think of the consequences of your actions.
iv) I wish you weren't so involved in your past glories. I wish you were more involved in the present. You're always thinking of the past!
v) I wish you would think of me (more/sometimes). I wish you didn't think more of your mother than you do of me.
vi) I wish you would think about the future. I wish you would try to plan ahead. I wish you were (more) realistic.
vii) I wish you would appreciate how hard I work. I wish you would think of me (more/sometimes).

The present progressive form can only be used in **i), ii)** and **iv)**.

13 **a)** big **b)** car **c)** toy **d)** basketball, baseball, football, tennis, rugby, running, swimming, etc.

14 First the generic word is given in the infinitive, then the past tense.
1) take out (took out) **2)** put (put) **3)** pull (pulled) **4)** breathe in (breathed in) **5)** open (opened) **6)** throw (threw) **7)** go (went) **8)** move (moved) the position of **9)** breathe (breathed) in **10)** breathe (breathed) out

15 **a)** turned on **b)** started (the car) **c)** opened and closed (hard), ran **d)** threw **e)** pulled **f)** turned **g)** made/pushed **h)** threw **i)** walked (slowly) **j)** get in, put

19 **1)** gazing **2)** squinting **3)** joined **4)** hammered **5)** muttered **6)** draining **7)** weakening **8)** crawl away **9)** squirted **10)** watch

20 The feeling of power and ability which Roy feels after moments of weakness is comparable to the remembered greatness that Ace feels at the end of Updike's story. Most people, and not only sportsmen, relive moments of past glory or importance.